Hello, it's Confidence Calling!

A Self-Confidence and Self-Esteem Workbook for Women

Overcome shyness, self-doubt, and anxiety for good!

Written by: Elena Wright

Elena Wright © Copyright 2019 - All rights reserved.

The content contained within this book may not be reproduced, duplicated or transmitted without direct written permission from the author or the publisher.

Under no circumstances will any blame or legal responsibility be held against the publisher, or author, for any damages, reparation, or monetary loss due to the information contained within this book, either directly or indirectly.

Legal Notice:

This book is copyright protected. It is only for personal use. You cannot amend, distribute, sell, use, quote or paraphrase any part, or the content within this book, without the consent of the author or publisher.

Disclaimer Notice:

Please note the information contained within this document is for educational and entertainment purposes only. All effort has been executed to present accurate, up to date, reliable, complete information. No warranties of any kind are declared or implied. Readers acknowledge that the author is not engaging in the rendering of legal, financial, medical or professional advice. The content within this book has been derived from various sources. Please consult a licensed professional before attempting any techniques outlined in this book.

By reading this document, the reader agrees that under no circumstances is the author responsible for any losses, direct or indirect, that are incurred as a result of the use of information contained within this document, including, but not limited to, errors, omissions, or inaccuracies.

Table of Contents

Introduction 7

Chapter 1 - Discover self-confidence and why it's worth developing 19

What is self-confidence? 20
What is self-esteem? 21
Why is self-confidence so important? 26
Small steps you can take right now to improve your self-confidence 30
Start your 30-day Recovery Plan Activities 31
Day 1-3 of your 30-day Recovery Plan 33

Chapter 2 - Observe Your Present Self to Move Forward without Judgment 37

Observing your current state of confidence 38
9 Common Signs that your confidence is dipping 42
Making Judgments...44
Does my self-esteem stem from my childhood? 46
The Psychology of Self-Confidence 48
What different behaviors suggest low self-esteem? 51
How quickly can I improve my self-esteem? 62
Days 4-6 of your 30-day Recovery Plan 63

Chapter 3 - Tackle Shyness to Present Your Authenticity in Any Crowd 67

What is shyness, how it develops and ways to move past it? 68
What's the difference between shyness and introversion? 70
Social anxiety and Shyness 73
Staying Authentic 74
Day 7-9 of your 30-day Recovery Plan 78

Chapter 4 - Move from Self-Doubt into Self-Trust to Solidify Your Internal Relationship ...81

Where does self-doubt come from? 82
Where does imposter syndrome come from? 84
What are self-limiting beliefs and how do we overcome them? ...86
How can I start to trust myself and instill self-belief? 89
Self-doubt versus living with solid self-trust 92
Day 10-12 of your 30-day Recovery Plan 94

Chapter 5 - Soothe Anxiety and Learn to "Recharge" Your Confidence 97

How symptoms of anxiety could be knocking your confidence 98
Effective rest and stress-relief strategies that help you control your anxieties 102
How can resting and taking care of myself help my confidence? ..105
How can I make changes to boost my energy levels? 107
Day 13-15 of your 30-Day Recovery Plan 110

Chapter 6 - Check Your Self-Image to Eliminate Tendencies of Comparison 115

What do we mean by 'self', what is self-image, and how is it formed and developed? 116

How comparing ourselves makes us unhappy and
gives our confidence a bashing 122
Self-esteem and confidence in a digital age 126
Day 16-18 of your 30-day recovery plan 129

Chapter 7 - Uncover the Negative Stories You Tell Yourself to Rewrite Your Inner Dialogue..133

We all have a story to tell our self, but how accurate are they? 134
How important are our internal stories?....................................136
How to observe your inner dialogue and rewrite it 139
Day 19-21 of your 30-day Recovery Plan 143

Chapter 8 - Build Self-Care Routines that Remind You of Your Worth 147

Self-care and why we need it 148
How to boost your self-worth 151
Feeling well-cared for versus feeling worthy 154
Are hobbies a type of self-care? 157
Days 22-24 of your 30-day Recovery Plan 158

Chapter 9 - Observe Improvements You've Made to Start Giving Yourself Credit for Progress 161

Big goals versus small goals 163
What if I don't know I've achieved something? 167
How should I celebrate my success? 170
Days 25-27 of your 30-day Recovery Plan 173

Chapter 10 - Establish Actions to Move Forward into a Life of Exuding with Confidence 175

Retaining confidence, even if there are setbacks 176

Establish a daily routine that boosts your
confidence and self-esteem 179

7 Tips to bounce back faster when you make mistakes 184

Negative emotions and how to deal with them 186

How to develop your resilience 188

Maintaining your ideal level of confidence and self-esteem 189

Days 28-30 of your 30-day Recovery Plan 192

Moving Forward... 193

Conclusion 197

Reference List 205

Introduction

"As soon as you trust yourself, you will know how to live."

Johann Wolfgang von Goethe

Do you trust your own actions and abilities? According to Johann Wolfgang von Goethe above, it's only then you can start to live your life. If you don't trust yourself to do something, how can you expect others to trust you? In life, people want you to make guarantees and assurances that you 'can', not that you 'might or think you can', especially in a professional capacity. It's difficult to suggest that you can certainly do something if you don't have that self-belief and self-worth.

As women we go through life comparing ourselves. We compare ourselves to other models in magazines, we compare ourselves to other wives and mothers, and we compare our careers, education and relationships. We want to be the best at everything, some women even want to be the best cook and compare themselves to others. Imagine a child going home after a playdate and telling her mom that the other kids mom makes the *best* cupcakes. Something like that can be a slap in the face but ultimately, if you feel threatened or upset by this comment, it's you who needs to change. Making nicer cupcakes does not make the other mom a better mother than you, nor does it make her a better cook. If those thoughts enter a person's mind – this is you doubting yourself and your mind processing this all wrong, because firstly, kids sometimes say some funny things they don't mean. They often exaggerate and it was probably a compliment because they had a great time. Next, that might be the only sweet thing your child has eaten today, and it was a treat, and finally, we all have different likes and dislikes; plus, we simply can't be the best at everything. This needs to be reframed – Sally's Mom (the other mom) makes good cakes, it's her strength. Also, your child just had a lovely time visiting her friend, so above all, this is a time for joy! Processing small events like this in an irrational way can damage your self-confidence, and this is something that some of us do on a regular basis, unknowingly.

Self-confidence and self-esteem are complex. They are a state of mind that attempt to define our thoughts and feelings, but they are difficult to control because they focus on ourselves. It is often difficult to see our own qualities, trust our own abilities, and to feel like we've made the best judgment call. We might even think about what we could've done, should've done, or would've done in certain situations, and we tend to beat ourselves up about it because we feel like we just didn't handle things well. *Does this sound familiar?* That is your self-doubt niggling away at you and it's bringing down your confidence, just like the cupcake example from earlier.

These feelings can affect us because the way we feel about ourselves often shapes the way we think and behave. If we feel like we're not good enough, this shows. How can we expect others to have faith in us, or believe we can do something, if we don't believe it of ourselves? Confident people are comfortable in their own skin but for someone who lacks confidence, this doesn't come naturally and for many people this rings a familiar sound of self-doubt.

Self-confidence and self-esteem can either be your best friend, or your worst enemy. If we allow it to control us in a negative way, it can affect everything we do. If we control it positively, we can rule the world and inspire others. Confidence can truly be the determining factor in what we do next in our life because it can mean success, or it can scupper our dreams. It influences the decisions we make in our personal lives, relationships, careers, and education.

Imagine you approach two self-confidence coaches to find out what they can do for you. You explain your situation and the first one says:

'I think I might be to help you to improve your confidence and self-esteem.'

The second tells you:
'I can help you to improve your confidence and self-esteem.'

Which one would you choose?

A coach costs a lot of money so most people wouldn't take a chance on someone who *might be able to* help them – they want someone who *can.* In order for that coach to say she CAN help, she shows one important thing; confidence in her own abilities! *How can someone teach you to be confident if they are not confident themselves?*

You're right, they can't and that's exactly why you would need a coach who believes in themselves to get the results you require.

Lacking in confidence can hold us back in life because we often end up doing things we don't want to do.

Maybe we were too shy to tell the boss that we couldn't work over tonight, so now we've agreed to it and now we feel anxious because we've had to arrange for someone to pick our kids up from school. Maybe we couldn't speak out about something because we felt so anxious and were afraid we'd make a fool of ourselves. We then spend so much time reflecting on these events, beating ourselves up because we didn't say no or handle it differently and this sets off all kinds of negative emotions. We regret that we didn't react differently.

As human beings, we don't like to have regrets. We have this idea of perfectionism in our head and anything less just isn't good enough. In reality, we set the standard so high that we are never going to be 'perfect' and by aiming for this, we are setting ourselves up for disappointment. Perfectionism is often part of the problem, because nobody is perfect.

Imagine you're at a conference and this amazing woman enters the speaking area. She looks happy, walks confidently, and she speaks so well, with ease, and it's like she's talking directly to you. She speaks to people at the reception afterwards and she is the ultimate socialite. You aspire to be her...

What if I told you that inside, just before the event, she was terrified? That a few years ago, she wouldn't have even attempted to board a stage or speak in front of so many people. A year ago, she was shy and anxious, and constantly beating herself up about what she DIDN'T do. *What if I told you that in order to get from the shy and anxious person she was, to the confident person she is today, was work on her own self-confidence and self-esteem?*

That doesn't mean she doesn't feel those exact feelings that you feel, it just means she doesn't allow them to control her. She's changed her thoughts on perfectionism; she gives herself a break, and she's altered how she feels about herself. She sees public speaking as a challenge and is willing to face her fear. She's also adopted a level of acceptance for herself and she knows that making mistakes is part of life. Even if things don't go to plan, she dusts herself off, learns from the experience and strives to do better next time. Working on herself, including her confidence and self-esteem has allowed her to become the person she is today and face her fears.

> *"To overcome fear is the quickest way to gain your self-confidence."*
>
> Roy T. Bennett, The Light in the Heart
> (Goodreads.com, 2020)[ii]

The point here is that everyone feels like you do from time to time, as we all have self-doubts or feel anxious but overcoming the fear by tackling it head on can boost confidence levels. These fearful feelings aren't unique, you just deal with them differently and by developing your self-confidence and self-esteem, you can learn to change your mindset and the way you deal with specific situations too. Our confidence and self-esteem are a projection of how we feel about ourselves so if we can start to see ourselves differently, we can better cope with the negativities that affect them.

Women have so many different roles and pressures in

their lives as we take on everything. We are daughters, wives, sisters, and mothers, but more and more women put pressure on themselves to excel in their career and education too. This is just the tip of the iceberg because women are warriors. We face every battle head on, and we are harsh on ourselves if we falter. Even if we do have confidence, we always want to do better and some of us can't shake that feeling of being an imposter – that we're just not good enough. It's because we take on so much, that we sometimes feel overwhelmed and our confidence can dip. Throughout this book, we will work on coping and self-belief strategies that will help you reframe your thoughts and change the way you think and handle situations. This will change how you see yourself.

When a person feels good about themselves it can really change how other people see them too because that confidence shines through. Many studies suggest that people who are confident and strive for success are more likely to achieve it. By working on ourselves, we can really start to focus on what we want in life and the things that make us happy. Shyness is such a common trait that it's often something that we don't consider as being a major barrier. However shyness can soon develop into anxiety too and this can damage our self-confidence.

In hindsight, shyness only becomes a barrier if we don't have the strength to overcome this. If we apply for a job and feel nervous about the interview because we don't know what we'll say, that's normal. If we don't apply because of these feelings, then this is a whole new level of shyness that can be damaging. Both the nervousness for the interview and the refusal to even apply for the job is often because the shyness has escalated and caused anxieties. Again, this impacts our levels of self-confidence.

If you would like to find your self-confidence and are ready to stop allowing your doubts, anxieties, and shyness to control your life, this book is for you. With this 30-day recovery plan you can start to work on yourself. This will lead you on a journey of self-discovery and help you build, repair and develop your confidence the right way.

It's time to change your life, and overcome those barriers, for good!

Chapter 1

Discover self-confidence and why it's worth developing

Have you ever wondered why you feel the way you do or why you doubt yourself? Often the way we judge ourselves isn't fair, because we are programmed to be hard on ourselves. We often have high expectations of ourselves, so we set goals and targets that we don't really think we can achieve. *So, why do we set them?* Basically, we set ourselves up to fail and as we don't like failure, this affects us and the way we feel about ourselves. Those feelings affect our self-confidence.

We fear failure when failure really isn't something to fear, it's something that we can embrace. You're probably thinking, *that's crazy,* but what if I told you that we can use it to help us develop and improve?

Would you like to stop being so hard on yourself and improve your self-belief? If so, you're ready to take the next step...

What is self-confidence?

Defining self-confidence isn't easy. Self-confidence is a feeling, but it's a feeling that can affect the person we are and how we think, act, or behave. It's the way we feel about ourselves and this differs from person to person. To put it simply, if you are self-confident, you believe in your own abilities, qualities, judgements and beliefs. If you aren't confident, you doubt yourself and don't believe in yourself, and this can have instrumental repercussions on what you do in your life. That means that when we do something, we question whether we did it correctly or effectively. We often assume that we won't do well, and this lack of confidence can affect our performance or our ability to handle specific situations. It can also affect how we feel, and this impacts how we live our life as we stop making changes and taking chances.

Our self-confidence influences our feelings and behavior. It can impact many things including our work life, relationships and even our family life. Those who lack confidence can face struggles with anxiety and sometimes end up doing things that they don't want to do because they are too anxious or shy to say no. They might get overlooked for that promotion because they are too afraid to speak out. They doubt their own abilities and make assumptions about themselves. For instance, they could meet the man of their dreams, but because of previous relationships failing, they believe that this relationship is doomed from the start. Due to this attitude and belief, their relationship can suffer because it's already defeated in the person's mind, so they don't accept it to succeed. In the movie, *Anger*

Management (Segal, 2003)[iii] the main character Dave was bullied as a child and particular events from his past cause him to almost lose the love of his life because he can't admit his feelings in public. Furthermore, his own fear of public embarrassment is what allows his boss to steal his design ideas. This comedy portrays how previous life events can affect the person we become. Luckily, after a series of crazy events, Dave overcomes his anxieties.

People who are confident stand out. People can rely on them because they know they will get an honest answer. They believe in themselves, and that shows in everything they do, and it encourages other people to believe in them too. Confidence brings charisma, and it's a success magnet. Theodore Roosevelt (Goodreads, 2019) once said, "Believe you can and you're halfway there."[iv] This is a true statement. If we don't believe, we allow our fear of failure to hold us back. This doesn't mean confident people never feel nervous or anxious, it just means they can cope with their feelings and they don't allow it to shape their thoughts and actions. People who lack confidence don't know how to handle those feelings and thoughts, and therefore aren't in control of their own success. This means they feel like they've failed before they begin – they accept defeat and therefore they allow themselves to be defeated easily. It's easy to become stuck in the rut of self-doubt but only those who take action to improve and work on themselves have the ability to climb out and flourish.

What is self-esteem?

Self-esteem is closely related to self-confidence, in fact it's part of it. Over the last 50 years there has been a major self-esteem movement, focusing on how it can be used to improve success, especially in children. When it comes to self-esteem, Positive Psychology claims that self-esteem is one of the basic human motivations from Maslow's hierarchy of needs and when the need is fulfilled, we grow and thrive. They suggest that there are three components that make up self-esteem.

This includes:

- It's an essential human need that ensures healthy development.
- It is automatically shaped from your personal beliefs.
- It can impact how we think, act, feel and behave (PositivePsychology.com, 2019)[v].

If someone has low self-esteem, they can be seen to have very little self-respect too. This is because they tend to make bad choices, often feel deflated or depressed and this can continue to have a negative impact in their life. People with low self-esteem can also fall into destructive relationships and many fall into this pattern over and over again. They don't feel an ounce of self-worth, they allow others to treat them badly because they feel that they deserve it. Of course, this is ridiculous!

If you have high self-esteem it can be just as destructive, so there has to be a realistic balance. It is not acceptable to live your life assuming that you're better than others or that the world owes you something; attitudes like this can ruin careers and relationships.

If we want to build and improve our self-esteem and self-confidence, we first need to work on ourselves and develop a level of self-acceptance. Only then can we achieve self-actualization, which helps us discover who we want to be and what we want in life. *So, what is that?* Well, self-actualization is having regular, powerful, valuable, and mind-blowing experiences that strengthen who we are. These experiences often mean that we have come to accept ourselves; we embrace opportunities, experiences and others, yet at the same time being realistic. When we achieve self-actualization, we are content and happy with our own company, but still, we like to have to have fun and don't feel restrained by society. They are still philosophical, autonomous and they are motivated by their values, ethics and responsibilities (Verywell Mind, 2020)[vi].

Why is self-confidence so important?

Sometimes, people have low self-confidence. This can be for numerous reasons, but it's often due to negative thought patterns that we allow to flow through our mind without question, as a result of beliefs we've formed over time. Sometimes events occur or some kind of anxiety is triggered, and this can also cause damage to our self-confidence. It's important to acknowledge these things, so that you can move forward and overcome the issues that have knocked down your confidence levels.

If your confidence levels are low, it can be really difficult to believe in yourself and get what you want out of life. It can instill a fear, and you stop believing that you can achieve your dreams and often many people with this fear settle for what they have. You may also need constant reassurance from others too, and this can affect the different relationships in your life. Others are drawn to happy, independent and confidence people who believe in themselves.

Self-confidence is so important because studies suggest that self-confident people are successful. There are many benefits of being self-confident and this can really shape our lives.

Self-confidence often means:

- Improved performance – When we are confident in ourselves and know we can do something well, we feel motivated. This often means that our performance is improved as we know we can do it and strive to be the best.

- Social ease – A confident person who is confident in their own skin is more relaxed in social situations. Their confidence and self-belief shine through in their personality and others often feel drawn to their charisma. That's because their positivity, energy and success acts as a magnet.

- Improved health – Studies suggest that good self-confidence and self-esteem indicate good mental health. That doesn't suggest that people who are confident do not have mental health issues, but just that they have the right tools to be able to cope and deal with situations that could stir up feelings of anxiety, self-doubt and shyness. It often fuels our social skills and these days, there is a lot of confidence building work in schools so that young people can adopt these tools from a young age. This can help them deal with exam and peer pressure.

- Happiness – If you feel good about yourself you are happy, and if you are happy, it can lead to you getting what you want out of life. A self-confident person isn't afraid of doing things that make them happy, as it's all part of taking care of themselves. This means that they feel in control as they recognize their own strengths and weaknesses, but while they play on their strengths, they work to develop and improve their weaknesses. Being happy and striving forward removes the fear. Fear is what prevents us from moving forward in live so with a positive attitude, you can be ready to face any obstacles head-on, because you aren't afraid to fail. You see failure as a change to learn something new or develop a skill, rather than stopping and feeling defeated.

- The ability to inspire others – Have you ever watched a person and thought, *wow, they are awesome?* They were confident and charismatic, and you felt a strong admiration. This could be a public speaker, or someone who is famous or well-known. Well that's a confident person and because their charisma and confidence shines, it inspires other people. Especially if they have a story to tell that you can relate too. We are constantly inspired by confident people, because let's face it, if someone sat quietly, was unsocial and didn't speak much, then how are you supposed to get to know them? Someone who is confident puts themselves out there and often displays a little vulnerability about their own life. Again, this inspires others and you could be a person that inspires other people if you build and develop your own self-confidence.

Small steps you can take right now to improve your self-confidence

This book will explore self-confidence, and help you develop your own over a longer period of time so that you can get what you want in life. There are some steps you can take right now to improve your confidence and self-esteem. Some of them, we will cover in more depth later, but if you want to make some small, fast changes, try these steps below:

- When you wake up in the morning, write down three things you are thankful for. It's time to do something different so if you usually sit quietly in a team meeting, barely speak to the coffee barista that serves you coffee, or you stand quietly in the playground away from the other parents, try something new. Speak! Say hello, comment about the weather, say something interesting or contribute to the team meeting and state your opinion or idea. This can make you feel happy and even proud of yourself.

- Spend some time every day on you. Taking care of yourself is important and even if it's something like reading, going for a walk, going for a coffee with your friend, or taking a long bath, it's important for your own health and happiness.

- Do something kind or help another person. Taking time away from ourselves and doing something for another can really help us to focus. Just taking some time to focus on something can help us to move away from our negative thinking patterns.

- Walk away, breathe and take a few moments to collect your thoughts. Sometimes we can be a little irrational when we aren't feeling confident as those feelings of anxiousness become too much. Sometimes a brisk walk, a chat with a friend or just some air can make a wealth of difference.

Start your 30-day Recovery Plan Activities

It's important to start making progress with your

confidence now, to see maximum results. That's why we've devised some steps for you each day for the next 30 days, so that you can start to work on yourself and slowly make changes and explore your confidence, then you can figure out what you want from life and what makes you happy.

Journaling is a huge part of this workbook as it has endless benefits, and it is suggested that you embrace this concept for the whole of the 30-days at least. Journaling has so many benefits because it can help you to feel calm, encourage you to solve issues and problems, it helps you make sense of your thoughts and actions, while gaining clarity, and it can also increase your creativity. Throughout this book we reflect on negative thought patterns and actions, so journaling will help you to track and monitor those patterns too. A key benefit of journaling is that it helps you get those thoughts out of your head and on paper. Many people report that if they journal in the evening before bed, they sleep better. That's because you are putting your thoughts and ideas on paper, so you don't have them swimming around your head all night. This way, you don't need to worry in case you forget them.

If you've never journaled before, don't worry. This guide will help you through each three-day cycle and provide prompts and ideas to help you journal with ease. Soon, it will become second nature!

Day 1-3 of your 30-day Recovery Plan

You may have heard of journaling before and it's a great way to start organizing your thoughts as it helps you to identify any problems and anything that holds you back.

START YOUR JOURNAL
Your first task is to start a journal and write in it for three days of your self-confidence journey. You can use the prompts below to reflect on what we've covered in chapter 1 if you aren't sure of what to write:
- What aspects of your self-esteem and self-confidence hold you back?
- Did any of the traits highlighted in the chapter resonate with you? Write them out.

- Write a description or profile of the person you aspire to be – think about what you would do if you weren't holding yourself back.
- How does it make you feel when your confidence is lacking?
- Are there any patterns in the way you think or act? Is this a new feeling or have you always felt like that? Are there any events that trigger how you feel?

Practice journaling in a style that suits you over the next 3 days.

ACTIONABLE STEP

Examine your journal after the first three days and see if you can see any patterns in the way you think or act. We all behave in a certain way, so this is normal.

Do something different to disrupt this pattern. For example, if you don't speak out at work or in meetings, try it. This is often empowering. *How did you feel after you disrupted the pattern?*

ACTIVITY

When we first start analyzing our behavior and thought patterns, they can be overwhelming. We might not know why we react in a particular way or why we aren't confident. Calming the mind is really important to this whole process.

If you start to feel overwhelmed, try this activity to calm you down. Earlier in this chapter, we talked about walking away and taking some time.

Relaxed breathing can really help with this:

- Take yourself off to somewhere quiet.
- Sit down, relax, and close your eyes.
- Breathe in for five seconds and out for seven.
- Try to clear your mind by concentrating on the rhythm.
- Repeat the words "I am worthy of taking up space" 3 times.
- Absorb the feeling of confidence for another 10 seconds.

Open your eyes and go back to whatever you were doing before.

Chapter 2

Observe Your Present Self to Move Forward without Judgment

It's said that we are our own biggest critic and it's true that we are often harsh on ourselves. We often don't consider using our critiquing abilities for the greater good, but when it comes to our confidence, this is certainly possible. You see, critiquing is in fact a skill, and there's a rule you must observe when critiquing your confidence levels… in order to critique effectively, you need to back up your findings with an observation or evidence.

If you're going to make judgments, you should be sure to justify it. Negative judgments can appear nasty, so it's important to communicate them in an effective and constructive way and always think of something positive to say!

Observing your current state of confidence

A person with low confidence often behaves in specific ways that gives us a clue about their current confidence level. Use the quiz below to assess your current state of confidence:

1. How easy do you make decisions? Are you…?
    a) *Indecisive.* I never know if I'm making the right decision and I can never decide whether I should or shouldn't do something.
    b) *Sometimes indecisive but other times I know what I want.* It depends on the situation as sometimes I know exactly what I want and other times I don't.
    c) *I know what I want and make decisions with ease.*

There is no self-doubt, you just make your decision and go for it.

2. If I have to speak in front of others or explain anything, I feel...
   a) *Flustered, and a little scared.* I dread these situations and worry about them for days.
   b) *Unsure.* I can usually put my worries in the back of my mind and focus on what I need to do. I still worry but I get on with it.
   c) *Excited.* I thrive in situations like this. I enjoy speaking in front of others.

3. How easily do you confront others?
   a) I don't, I avoid it. I only do this if absolutely necessary, but it provokes emotion.
   b) *I do it in the nicest way possible, often apologizing beforehand and after.*
   c) *I put my professional head on, plan what I should say, and speak confidently about the matter.*

4. If I fail, I...
   a) *Give up.* I knew it was going to fail, it's my own fault.

b) *Think, "at least I tried". I talk it through with someone and eventually I might try again.*

c) *Consider the experience a learning curve. I analyze where I went wrong, ask advice from others, and I try again.*

5. You are asked to do something difficult that you've never done before. You say...
   a) *I can't.*
   b) *I'll give it a go.*
   c) *I'll do it.* Then you ask lots of questions.

Mostly A:

You need to work on your confidence issues as they are currently holding you back. You are in danger of self-doubt controlling everything you do, but now it's time to start moving forward. Everyone around you knows that great things are ahead of you, but you currently don't see your own worth. You need to believe in yourself and increase your confidence as eventually, people could stop reminding you. You're the master of your own destiny – write a list of everything you know, and I mean EVERYTHING. You might even surprise yourself!

Mostly B:

You have some confidence issues and although they hold you back, they aren't too overwhelming at this time. You do try to make a stand and control your self-doubt, but you haven't mastered this yet. You are in danger of allowing confidence issues to escalate, so it's really important that you keep developing your confidence. Take some time to clear your mind and relax, so you can start to see what you really want in life. Set some goals for yourself and start pushing – if you really want something, you need to grab it with both hands. Keep building, growing and learning – don't back down or give up because what you want is within reach.

Mostly C:

Your confidence levels are good, and you have a good attitude that will help you grow and develop. Just be careful that you maintain those confidence levels as they will help you get what you really want in life. There are some great ways you can work on maintaining your confidence and even though you're doing well, don't stop setting goals and striving for more. It's important that you schedule in some time for yourself too, to ensure you're heading for what you really want. Don't be afraid to reassess what you want and if you change your mind, that's fine – we're allowed to change our course. Ensure you aren't too hard on yourself too, as this can be damaging to your confidence. Reach for the stars, we know you've got this!

You've done the quiz, so you know what level your confidence is at presently – but what other signs indicate that you have low self-esteem? Many people don't even notice when their confidence is slipping, so here are some common signs.

9 Common Signs that your confidence is dipping

When your confidence is starting slip, it's hard to initially recognize the signs. One minute, everything is going fine, and before you know it things have spiraled out of control. We can prevent this spiral if we are aware of some of the signs. A dip in confidence can start with a feeling of unease, or anxiousness, at a gradual rate.

These feelings can stem from feeling nervous about something and they creep up on you.

The 9 most common signs are:
- Backing down in a disagreement, just because it's easier and it avoids conflict. We can do this even if we are right, but we can't face a draining argument, or we're worried that we don't get our point across effectively.
- If someone makes a constructive comment to help you, you find yourself emotional or upset; you see these things as a personal attack, even though your rational mind knows they are not.
- You like to have your make-up done or hair done and can't answer the door or leave the home if you're not at a specific standard.
- When you're in a social situation, you'd rather check your phone every couple of minutes than talk to others.
- When someone pays you a compliment, you shy away because you don't know how to react.
- It's difficult for you to make decisions, even simple ones. You change your mind constantly.

- You don't like to voice your own opinion because you're afraid that anything you say would not be valid.
- You tend to self-sabotage your own chances, because you always feel unworthy and feel like another person (often anyone) is more suitable for a specific task than you are. You compare yourself to them and think of reasons why you shouldn't do things.
- When you don't succeed on your first attempt, you stop or give up because you feel like you're not going to be successful anyway, so you should quit sooner rather than later (Lifehack, 2020)[vii].

Making Judgments

We've talked a lot about being naturally hard on ourselves and it's time to think a little more about that. We can sometimes make judgments or assumptions based on our own beliefs or also depending on how we feel, but it's important to refrain from making judgments when exploring confidence. Making judgments and assumptions can be toxic. If your confidence is low already and you start shooting yourself down further, it could lead to further issues, like depression, and you may even give up or stop working on your confidence. Confidence is complex and it's closely linked to self-belief, self-esteem, self-worth, as well as anxiety and other mental health conditions. It is often a tiny piece of a thousand-piece puzzle, but without it, you are not complete. Improving our confidence can be the final piece when improving our mind, body and spirit, but until we understand its make-up, and how we can develop or improve it, we should never make judgments regarding others or ourselves because issues could be embedded much deeper. Judgments and assumptions are often the root of the demise of confidence, so bear that in mind as you continue exploring yours.

Judgments are often the foundations we use for decision-making and while it's important not to dwell on the judgments of others, you still need to make judgments in your own life. In order to make a justified judgement, you need to pay attention to both sides – the positives and negatives. You should also be aware of the impact your judgment will have – *would somebody lose their job because you made a judgment about their work ethics?* It's important that you take an outside perspective and listen to the views of others. Ensure you know your topic and receive any advice or guidance as needed – there's never any harm in asking others to help or contribute.

By making judgments, we become accountable for actions or decisions. Taking responsibility is a massive step if confidence is low, so don't be afraid to ask for support if needed.

Does my self-esteem stem from my childhood?

Many people question whether their self-esteem issues are embedded from childhood, and this is a good, yet complex question. We do carry many beliefs from our childhood, and it can be difficult to change them into something positive. If we were made to feel inadequate as a child, then this feeling of worthlessness can hold us back in the future. It can mean we don't take certain opportunities throughout our lives because we don't want to be embarrassed or made to feel unworthy again.

It is suggested that children have high self-esteem and low self-esteem can be related to physical punishment or a lack of affection or love from their family. That does not mean that this is the only reason. A child who is generally unhappy or is bullied
can have low self-esteem too and it can also result in in them treating others unfairly too. Children with low self-esteem can withdraw themselves and often struggle socially, which can also become a problem in adulthood. They often do not have fun and lack confidence in fear of being ridiculed. As they fear failure, they quit things easily, cheat, avoid situations they don't like and some even turn into bullies as they adopt negative coping strategies.

In teenagers, self-esteem can also dip and sometimes this is in relation to puberty and body image. Obviously, when teenagers start to experience feelings due to hormone changes, they have to learn to cope with these and it can take some time to control feelings and emotions. As their bodies change, they can also start to consider pictures in magazines as being the ideal and if they feel they need to look like that, it can make them feel low about themselves. Teenagers are vulnerable and influenced easily. If they struggle to feel good enough or comfortable with themselves and their own body, it can cause their self-esteem to plummet.

Inevitably, if you did not deal with these issues as a child, then you will take them with you into adulthood. The longer you believe the beliefs ingrained into you as a child, the more difficult it is to change them. But it's not impossible! (Mcleod, 2012)[viii].

The Psychology of Self-Confidence

It's obvious that some people struggle with self-confidence while others don't, *but why is that?* In truth, self-confidence is a personal, individual thing, because it's the way we view ourselves and it has a lot to do with how we personally feel. Many things can contribute to how we feel or view ourselves. Our genes, culture, and all other circumstances that we live through, such as bullying, abuse (mental and physical), and trauma can influence our self-confidence. It's whether we can work through them and make the difference, that matters.

Many studies suggest that some self-confidence traits are programmed in us since birth. They have focused on genetics and how the chemicals in our brain make a difference to self-confidence. We can have different serotonin (which is said to stimulate happiness) and oxytocin (the cuddle hormone) levels, which can mean we adopt different personality traits and it's those that impact whether or not confidence is inherited. Obviously, those with higher self-esteem levels produce those happy hormones in the brain (Psychology Today, 2018)[ix]. There are many studies that highlight the neuroscience behind this idea as they suggest that people who demonstrate several low self-esteem traits, suffer more social pain from social exclusion. People who demonstrate higher levels of self-esteem, suffer less social pain from social exclusion (Onoda et al.,

2010)[x]. This is because they are generally happier and have stronger coping mechanisms to deal with any exclusions.

Sometimes we don't understand the rules of self-confidence because we've never been taught them and often this is because our heads have been filled with the wrong information. For example, if we were brought up to think that only being perfect is acceptable, it can cause a major impact on our lives. In truth, nobody is perfect! Often, other things can affect our self-confidence too, and it's often that feeling of not fitting in, which could be down to things like gender, age, sexual orientation and race. If you've ever been discriminated against or humiliated, it can become increasingly difficult to feel comfortable with yourself as you struggle to belong. The world itself is also to blame, as everyone struggles with self-doubt now and then, and often messages portrayed in the media can make us feel inadequate too. Let's not forget that self-confidence issues can also be linked to depression and anxiety too (Psychology Today, 2018)[xi].

All these feelings and beliefs influence the way we perceive the world, and the way we think it perceives us. This all contributes to the way we view ourselves and this impacts our self-confidence. Self-confidence is complex, so it's not easy to understand. Our mind is programmed to think for itself based on our beliefs that shape it. If we can start to understand where our self-confidence issues stem from, we can certainly try to develop and improve this. Increasing self-confidence could change the way you view life and yourself, which could mean you improve your mental health and change your negative beliefs. This can ultimately enrich your life, career and relationships in the longer term.

What different behaviors suggest low self-esteem?

Low confidence and self-esteem can certainly trigger certain emotions or behaviors. We've talked about the signs of low-confidence earlier in this book, but we've been reflecting on what indicates low self-esteem in this chapter. There are some behavioral signs that can suggest you are lacking self-esteem. Below we're going to take a quick look at these behaviors and make some suggestions of how we can alter these to improve confidence and self-esteem. We have mentioned some of these already, but it's time to address and dig deep in their meaning.

Avoidance behaviors certainly signal low self-esteem. This includes quitting, avoiding situations or people, and even procrastinating or struggling to concentrate can all indicate this. This is because these behavior types stem from your fear of failure, which is part of your belief system. Since we don't like to fail, we would rather not try. Avoiding situations, people or events, means you protect yourself, as you don't want to suffer with those negative thoughts and feelings that you feel when you think you've failed (Counselling-directory.org.uk, 2016)[xii].

So, what can we possibly do to change this? Well, we need to change how you feel about failure. You see, many people view failure as a learning curve. I want you to think about when we are babies and we learn to walk. Walking takes practice, but we don't give up, we keep going until we can do it. Or talking. It takes years of practice to perfect our speech capabilities, but we don't simply stop trying. If we had this attitude about failure all of our life, we would never learn anything. To want to learn is a good thing, it's how we grow and develop. Next time, if you want to avoid a situation, think, *what you can do to make that more comfortable? What do you need to do or learn? Can you make a plan and some actionable steps of how you can face this fear?*

Perfectionist behaviors can also signal low self-esteem. If you work hard in an excessive way, you like to control everything, you're extremely competitive, like to try and please others, and act angry if things don't go your way, then you are showing perfectionist behaviors. If someone is a perfectionist, they feel that only being perfect is acceptable, and they believe they will only feel better about themselves if they meet the perfect category. They often make this impossible though, by setting goals that are unrealistic, thereby in reality, a perfectionist sets themselves up for failure. This is a huge problem, because they then feel frustrated and useless (Counselling-directory.org.uk, 2016)[xiii].

In truth, nothing is perfect, and everyone makes mistakes. Ideas of perfectionism are often false. Now, it's important to still aim big, but try this strategy to change your viewpoint of perfectionism, next time when you're completing a task.

- Think about what you want to achieve – what's your best target?
- Now work backwards. What would be the worst thing that could ever happen in relation to this task? What would be disastrous?
- Think about your next target which is a step down from best. What would be a good target?
- Finally, think about your next target down from 'good'. What would be an okay target for you? What could you live with?

Now the idea here is to aim for the best but you should also accept the good and okay targets as well as think about what you could've done to improve those. How could you reach your best target? What improvements can you make to do better next time? It's very rare that the worst-case scenario will happen, so be thankful for that. If it does, it's important that again you assess why it happened and what you can change to make sure it doesn't happen again. If you constantly assess, and think about what you can do to improve, it changes your whole perspective on how you view perfectionism.

Hiding is another type of behavior that indicates low self-esteem. Now this doesn't mean hiding as in the same essence of hide and seek but hiding your real self. For example, you hide your beliefs, sexual orientation, appearance, your likes or dislikes or even religion, weaknesses and certain characteristics about yourself. It's important to consider why we feel the need to hide ourselves. For instance, if you avoid telling your family that you no longer want to be a doctor and have changed your college major because you don't want to upset them, you are hiding your true self from them. You do this to avoid conflict, to help you fit in, to prevent negative criticism or simply to please others. However, pretending to be someone else damages your own self-esteem and confidence because you are suppressing yourself (Counselling-directory.org.uk, 2016)[xiv].

A person who has higher levels of confidence copes with the idea of judgement or disappointing others in a different way, because they accept that they can't hide who they are. It can be difficult to change this belief because we can never determine how the world will respond to us and there are some judgmental people out there.

Remember that if you hide yourself for acceptance or to please others, then it stems from a deep-rooted fear that others will be disappointed in you or not accept you. A confident person is happy and comfortable with who they are, so what other people think may of course be important but it's not everything. If you aren't true to yourself and others, you're being fake and lying to yourself. This means it's impossible for you to be happy.

To deal with this, write down some beliefs that others think or have of you, then write down the truth. Write down the best thing that would happen and the worst-case scenario and assess them. *Is the worst really that bad?* If you fear people falling out with you, that could be a short-term thing while they get over the initial shock of what you've been hiding. Others may respond a lot better than you think because people are increasingly acceptant of others and want you to be, or do, whatever makes you happy. Whatever you think the worst case is, it probably wouldn't last forever, but neither will your hiding – the truth comes out eventually. Many people respect you for telling the truth. You need to really stress to yourself that your happiness comes first (within reason of course), and the important people will accept it. Facing the judgments, or disappointments felt by others is better than living a lie.

Passive behaviors are when you just can't say no, even when you don't want to do something or can't fit it in. Saying no is hard, and you may find that you dismiss your own needs and thoughts, avoid expressing your opinion, and put yourself down regularly because you doubt your own abilities and judgments (Counselling-directory.org.uk, 2016)[xv].

We can all be passive and again, this is because we don't like to disappoint others. If we constantly say yes and do things that we don't want to or can't do, it can really affect us. Self-esteem means demonstrating the strong side of yourself, so in order to do that, you need to say no from time to time. If passive behavior is one of your traits, write down three occasions when you've said yes, when you really needed to say no, and think about how this affected you.

Write down how you would've liked to respond but ensure it's in a positive way as we don't need to get held back by the negative. Also, don't apologize! It's easy for someone to start saying things like *'I'm sorry, but I can't...'*

Why are you sorry?

Remember, you have a right to your own thoughts and feelings so own them. Speak your mind and don't doubt yourself.

Write down a list of phrases you can use to turn someone down next time they ask you to do something you just can't or don't want to do. Planning ahead is key here because you are no longer put on the spot and feel obliged to say yes. Saying no shows strength and confidence – you've got this!

Attention-seeking behaviors Sometimes when people suffer with low self-esteem or confidence, they behave in a way that grabs the attention of others. For example, they may behave in ways that are risky or dangerous, try to get sympathy from others, seek compliments from others, request reassurances from others that they are doing the right thing, or they may believe they aren't capable of doing certain things so they ask someone else to do it for them. A lot of these may come from the belief that they are not good enough, others are better, or they may need constant reassurances to make themselves feel better (Counselling-directory.org.uk, 2016)[xvi].

To avoid attention seeking behavior, you really need to assess yourself and write a list of the attention seeking behaviors you show. Next time you find yourself seeking compliments or reassurances from others, stop and give yourself one. Think about why you behave in a particular way and write some affirmations about believing in your self – you don't need others to react (in a positive or negative way), so focus on self-belief, rather than the beliefs of others. If you react in a risky or dangerous way, then you may need to get some help to work through your problems. Don't be afraid to get some help if you need it!

Aggressive behavior is another sign. Sometimes people with low confidence or self-esteem can react in an aggressive way as they try to fill in the gap, where their self worth and self-esteem is missing. Acting aggressively can be putting people down, shouting, and demanding things, and they can often blame others for the negative thoughts or feelings they have.

While jealousy to a certain level can be healthy, because it means you want to strive to have more for yourself, being jealous of others can also be toxic and can indicate a low level of self-esteem. A person with low self-esteem can struggle with developmental feedback or criticism too because they take it negatively, rather than regarding it as a learning experience or something to develop. Self-confidence and self-esteem have a lot to do with how we view and feel about ourselves (Counselling-directory.org.uk, 2016)[xvii].

Aggressive behavior isn't a great trait to suffer from because it can certainly hold you back as it portrays you in a negative light. Keep a diary of any aggressive behavior to monitor this and write down how you feel. Sometimes people just need to be aware of their aggressive behavior and they can come up with techniques to deal with it. Breathing exercises are a great way to calm yourself and clear your mind, but if you find that you feel a lot of anger and resentment, don't be afraid to seek professional medical help as there could be an underlying issue that is driving your low confidence and self-esteem. People under stress or depression can certainly act out, so keep a diary, try some breathing techniques and monitor how you feel. Seek medical help if it's out of control.

If some of the behaviors above link to how you react, this means you are starting to grow an awareness of how your low self-esteem and confidence is affecting you. When you're aware, you can start to monitor this and once you can monitor, you can improve and challenge those thoughts and behaviors.

How quickly can I improve my self-esteem?

There is no simple answer to this question. Self-esteem can be something that we need to work on regularly, if not constantly. While there are some quick fixes to self-esteem as soon as you become aware of the signaling behaviors, it may take a lot more time to get to the root of the problem.

If you read the list of behaviors in the previous section, and you relate to many of them, it can become overwhelming. With that in mind, you need to remember one key point – *every small change or step is progress.* It's a good idea to start changing your behaviors slowly, one at a time, and cement your new way of thinking before you move onto the next. This is suggested to be a healthier way as you are less likely to fail. To work on yourself at a slow pace requires patience, and for someone with low self-esteem, this isn't as simple as it sounds. You deserve the time, effort and dedication so stay motivated.

This leads to my next question, *what motivates you to succeed?* There must be something and this something might be the key to succeeding when it comes to increasing your self-esteem.

Days 4-6 of your 30-day Recovery Plan

JOURNALING

How's your journaling going? Journaling should be part of your daily routine but if you're struggling, start to think about what we've covered in chapter 2 in relation to self-esteem and the behaviors we display.

PROMPT: *Is there anything I did today that caused a reaction, that I would do differently?*

*Highlight behavior episodes that indicate your low

self-esteem. Use a highlighter or different colored pen to make them stand out (just put a small squiggle or star close to your notes), so you can spot them easily.

ACTIONABLE STEP

Review your journal and choose two or three reactions/behaviors to analyze. Start by putting them into a table:

- What behavior did you exhibit?
- What triggered this/what happened?
- How did you feel/react?
- How do you feel you should've reacted?
- What would be the best/worst possible outcome?
- How can you change this behavior/response or what would you do differently next time?

ACTIVITY – Plan to change

Look at your behaviors and look for patterns – are any behaviors similar to the different types discussed in chapter 2 (hiding, aggressive, passive etc…)?

Choose one behavior type that you feel holds you back

the most or is the most destructive and focus on that one. *For example, if you exhibit hiding behaviors, list the hiding behaviors that you've shown over the last few days. This could be holding you back because you feel anxious.*

Think about the types of situations that attract this behavior from you and plan a new response. Maybe you've hidden one of your skills at work or are hiding the fact you're completing a degree, in case people judge you or embarrass you, or ask you something you don't know. *Write how you do respond and write out how you want to respond.*

Finally, write out the best and worst outcome of this. For example, people could congratulate you and wish you well (best). Someone tells you degrees are a waste of time, they never needed one (worst), or goes on a rant about degrees being a waste of money. Regardless – does that really matter? Assess the worst outcome with the best. *Is the worst that bad? How will you respond?* Planning in advance is key to your success, so you aren't put on the spot.

Plan to make a small behavior change and when you achieve it, be proud – journal about it and how it made you feel!

Chapter 3

Tackle Shyness to Present Your Authenticity in Any Crowd

Do you ever want to hide, or maybe you want the ground to open up and swallow you? At least that would get you away from the situation you've found yourself in, right?

Well that's all fine but sadly, hiding will never solve your shyness issues...

It's common to be shy, especially when meeting new people, but shyness can really hold us back. Shyness sometimes means we don't introduce ourselves to others, so it can affect us on a social level. It can impact our job interviews, relationships, the way we work, and it can make us feel anxious. If we are shy, we tend to melt into the background of everything and we try not to draw attention to ourselves. When we do, it's extremely embarrassing! The problem is this shyness holds us back and stops us from getting the best out of ourselves. *But what is exactly is shyness and how can we overcome this for good?*

What is shyness, how it develops and ways to move past it?

Shyness is a part of our personality, in fact it's a personality trait. People who are shy, do not introduce themselves or communicate as quickly or as confidently as someone who is not shy or is confident. This is because they hesitate. They may have anxiety or they could worry: *Will I say the right thing?* Or *what should I say?* And they often just need that little extra time to think and gather themselves.

Shyness is a normal part of our personality, but the level of shyness can depend on our personal temperament. Sometimes people are extremely shy, and this can develop further by escalating stress and anxiety levels that can cause extreme anxiety. It can then grow into a social anxiety disorder if we don't work on this.

If you enter a room and you don't introduce yourself right away, it becomes harder and harder to make that initial introduction. Maybe you pull out your phone, pretend you're reading, or on your phone, and maybe you slip out of social gatherings as early as possible. Imagine this… you go to a networking meeting for your organization and you constantly check your phone, you put your head down, avoid talking to others, and you say very little. You can feel yourself going red and you slip out the back way. *Was it worth going?* Not really! It would be a waste of time and completely unproductive because you didn't make that initial introduction and became so anxious that you couldn't introduce yourself at all. It got harder the longer it went on until you left.

The more we allow ourselves to be shy, the more we allow it to fester, the more overwhelmed we feel and the harder it is to overcome. One of the ways to overcome shyness is to face to situations that make us feel shy, but on a controlled level. The idea is that you should take things slowly and not give up but celebrate the small wins along the way. Once we make progress and our confidence grows, our shyness will become easier to control.

What's the difference between shyness and introversion?

There are a lot of links made between introversion and shyness. This is because both can influence the way we communicate with others or the actions we take. If you're shy or an introvert, then you probably aren't as social as others. Some studies suggest that a key difference is that people who are shy, don't choose to feel as socially awkward when it comes to communicating with others, while an introvert has a choice. Someone who is shy may find it really difficult to communicate with others and this can actually start to make them feel anxious. An introvert doesn't get anxious when it comes to interacting with others, but they just don't particularly like or want to interact or communicate (Curtin, 2018)[xviii].

While shyness can be linked to anxiety and you do become introverted, the two are very different. Sometimes people are not sure whether they are shy, an introvert or an extrovert, but this is a very good question… We already know that to be shy, you feel anxious about social and communicative situations, and you can't control how you feel.

According to *Introvert Dear (2019)*, you're more of an introvert if you like being alone and having time for inner reflection, if socializing drains you both mentally and physically, if you enjoy writing and often prefer thinking to talking. An introvert often prefers to have deep relationships, so long-term friends or partners are common, rather than casual ones. Although an introvert is an excellent listener, they expect this in return and tend to look at life from the inside out. *Does this sound more like you?*

If you're more of an extrovert, then you get your energy from others and thrive on the social aspects in life as being alone brings you down. An extrovert is also interested in the world and is more of a talker rather than a listening – they think at their best when they are speaking. Extroverts often convey themselves in a more confident way as they can express themselves well, verbally, they are friendly and assertive, and they always keep themselves busy. *Does this sound more like you?* (Introvert, Dear, 2019)[xix].

There are no right or wrong answers here as often, people are a combination of the two, while others lean more towards one or the other. This is part of who you are, and many things can influence this including your energy, life, work and upbringing. Your beliefs, experiences and general view of the world can also shape our personality and temperament. *So, why do we need to know this?* In truth, it isn't essential but knowing our personality and temperaments can help us to understand who we are and how we can change. If we understand why we do something, or why we behave in a particular way, it becomes easier to make sense of everything, identify anything negative, and make that change.

Social anxiety and shyness

Social anxiety is another condition associated with shyness. Shyness can trigger feelings of anxiety due to the way a person feels about a social situation. We've already discussed shyness and how it is a personality trait; it's part of who we are, but social anxiety is very different.

Social anxiety is a severe anxiety disorder that prevents a person from partaking in certain activities and situations, because they can't control their levels of anxiety. This means they avoid even some of the most regular activities. A person who suffers from this disorder have a significant amount of fear. They feel embarrassed or humiliated when it comes to social based situation, especially if they feel that they will be expected or even pressurized to take part. When a person suffers severely from this it increases stress and distress levels, which means the person would much rather avoid the situation than feel this level of fear.

Like shyness, social anxiety disorder isn't a choice but there are things we can change or adopt to improve its impact. If you suffer from either, there are coping techniques you can use to ease the feelings of anxiousness, such as the breathing exercises we started looking at in chapter 1.

Staying Authentic

It's important to remember that when changing your personality, you're in danger of changing who you are. For some, this may seem to be good thing, but for others, they may not want to change too much – quite right! You may need to change certain aspects of yourself, providing you are changing for the right reasons, but it's important to stay true to who you are.

When you start to make changes it's important that you don't try to mold your personality to suit others. If we try to be something we're not it will make us unhappy which will cause further anxiety.

When others see you, they will see a sincere person when you are being yourself, but when you try to be something or someone you're not, you will find that people are not so easily fooled. It's in our nature to see through people and we are naturally drawn to authentic and honest people who we can relate to.

Be careful not to force any changes and only change aspects of yourself. If you are not true to yourself, cracks will appear and then others will struggle to trust you. We have to accept that although we can make improvements and slight changes, we can only be ourselves. However, this is something that many people with low-confidence struggle with. This is because they feel like they are not good enough.

If you are shy or anxious, then it is part of your personality trait. If you suddenly stop being shy, people will wonder why. That's because we don't just transition from being a quiet little mouse in the corner who daren't speak, into a loudmouth, overnight. Most people will never transition in such a drastic way, nor would anyone believe it because it's too unbelievable. Whilst it's great to make personal leaps in our personal development, ensure that you are still the person you are and want to be. To do this, you should:

- Visualize your ideal self and keep working towards it.
- Make the changes you need to make, for yourself.
- Don't make the changes you feel you should make, or that other people tell you to make.
- Think about your core beliefs in life and follow them. Don't stray!

With all of the conditions we've compared in this chapter, it is clear that there are similarities between social anxiety, shyness, and introversion. They can have similar traits as we've discovered but they are all very different too. So, *how do we take action to improve our confidence when there's so many things to overcome?*

There are a variety of techniques that we will unravel throughout this book and as every person is different, it's a case of trying them and seeing which works best for you.

If you suffer from shyness and social anxiety, you need to focus on changing your negative thinking patterns and you should also set yourself little challenges, so you can make progress. For example, you can use affirmations and goal setting to help yourself overcome your barriers. Your goals should be focused around engagement and trying new things. You can also use breathing strategies to learn how to cope in uncomfortable situations too. Obviously, it depends on the levels of your shyness and social anxieties, but make sure you celebrate any wins, no matter how small they are. Don't be afraid to get help and advice from professionals if you need it.

When it comes to introversion, you can use similar techniques, like goal setting and trying new things. If you are simply an introvert, it's likely that you won't need to do the coping techniques because if you are an introvert, this is usually a choice or preference. Again, make sure you celebrate your wins. As an introvert, it is likely that you don't like to draw attention to yourself but think about the type of person you would like to be and use small goals to make those personality changes. It is likely that you'll have to work on your own beliefs and attitude to help you take a different view and react differently to social situations. If you keep practicing social interactions and setting small goals, you will soon overcome this barrier as it will become second nature in the future.

Day 7-9 of your 30-day Recovery Plan

CONTINUE JOURNALING – Day 7-9
How is your journaling going? You're a week in now, so journaling should be part of your routine now. Make sure that journaling logs both your positive and negative experiences from the week.

*Spend some time reflecting on your first week of journaling. *Did you manage to change or disrupt one of* *your behavior patterns?*

ACTIONABLE STEP

During days 7-9, you're going to take some small steps to discovering your ideal self. Follow the steps for each day, below:

- Day 7 – Describe the personality of your ideal self. Are they confident? Happy? What do they like? How do they handle uncomfortable situations?
- Day 8 – Reflect on your ideal self. Think about you now. What do you need to do to transform into that ideal person? Set yourself 3-5 goals here.
- Day 9 – Spend some time reflecting on the last 8 days and keep your ideal self in mind. Think about difficulties you've faced and identify how you handled this. *Would you do anything different? How did you react? How should you react?* If you reacted well, be proud! Ask yourself, *how would the ideal me respond to this, what would they do?* Don't just look at the bad situations, look at the good too!

ACTIVITY

We've talked about our ideal self but think about who you are now.

Consider the points below:
- *What do you really want or need?*
- *Are you shy, an introvert, or socially anxious?*
- *Imagine yourself in an awkward situation that you usually avoid. Write a list of how you feel and how you would react in this situation.*
- *Make a list of three things you would like to change in your life.* This can be to do with jobs and careers, having more family or personal time, self-care, anything personal, material items, relationships.

Analyze your list and consider if any of these display traits of being an introvert, being shy, or socially anxious. Think about how your traits hold you back and really think about how you can overcome any barriers.

Keep hold of your list as it's an important part of your recovery!

Chapter 4

Move from Self-Doubt into Self-Trust to Solidify Your Internal Relationship

"The moment you doubt whether you can fly, you cease for ever to be able to do it."

J. M. Barrie, Peter Pan (Goodreads.com, 2020)[xx]

We all feel self-doubt from time-to-time, but have you thought about the impact this can have if it escalates?

As soon as we doubt ourselves, the trouble begins. As *J. M. Barrie* says above, as soon as we doubt, we may never be able to undo it. Now while that sentiment isn't wholly true, it is harder to fix feelings of self-doubt once they've occurred. Feelings of self-doubt can quite easily spiral out of control and once we've had them, the more difficult it becomes to remove them from our mind. This is all connected to the relationship we have with ourselves. Self-doubt is an internal barrier that some people feel daily and it prevents us from moving forward. After all, if you don't have trust in yourself or you doubt your own capabilities, *how can you expect anyone else to believe in you?*

Where does self-doubt come from?

It's human nature to question ourselves and our own abilities. We always wonder if we're good enough or qualified enough, and we often believe there is someone out there who is better than us. We put ourselves down and we believe these knee-jerk reactions and thoughts. Human nature makes us sell ourselves short but really, to be a specialist in a particular area, we just need to know more than the other people we're working with or speaking to. For instance, if you attend a meeting about the rainforest, the guest speaker would know more about the rain forest and the problems it faces than you do. They may not know everything, but we would count them as being an expert in that area. Even though that's how we view others, a lot of people struggle to see themselves as an expert in their field. Even if you don't know it yet, there will be something that you are a specialist or expert in!

Self-doubt ultimately comes from the relationship we have with ourselves. Think about how many times you question your actions and feelings… You probably can't remember the exact number of times you question yourself, but this can increase over time and it can set in feelings of panic. One way to monitor self-doubt is to note the event and what happened down in your journal.

Self-doubt is all about the way we view our own worth and how harsh we are with ourselves. Even the most qualified and experienced person in the world can feel uncomfortable in their own skin and often feel like an imposter. You might have heard of imposter syndrome before...

Where does imposter syndrome come from?

Imposter syndrome is an internalized fear. This term is often used in psychology to describe a lack of self-belief in ourselves and our own achievements. Many famous people and instrumental figures have admitted to suffering from imposter syndrome. It's more common than you think, but up until recently, people didn't really admit to this. This is because they were afraid to own up to this fear publicly because nobody likes to show weakness.

The admission of major public figures suffering with imposter syndrome recently has really brought to light just how common it is. Michelle Obama admitting this was surprising for many people – *How on earth can a former First Lady feel like she's an imposter?* But the truth is, anyone can feel like this. When speaking at a school, Michelle was told she was seen as 'a beacon of hope' and she admitted that her imposter syndrome never goes away, and she sometimes can't believe that people are really there to listen to her (Impostor Syndrome, 2020)[xxi].

There are now different perspectives on this, because showing a vulnerability keeps us human and it shows that no matter who we are: movie stars, entrepreneurs, public figures, sports stars, or political marvels, showing a little vulnerability grounds them. They are people, just like us and we share this trait. The fact that they can speak about this motivates us and gives us hope – if they can do it, so can we!

Imposter syndrome often comes from our core beliefs. Look at the statements below:
- *I've never been one of the popular kids.*
- *People who live in my neighborhood never make millions.*
- *Nobody in my family has ever studied in higher education.*

If you are brought up to believe any of the statements above or something similar, the likelihood is, you will believe this for most of your life... unless you take action to change these beliefs.

While some people suggest that imposter syndrome is a personality or character trait of a person, it can hold you back and it can bring on anxiety issues because imposter syndrome instils fear. Sometimes despite our experience and qualifications in life, we just don't feel good enough and we fear being exposed as a fraud. While this isn't a disorder, it is an internal belief in which people believe they do not deserve success. They simply categorize their successes as being good luck or being in the right place at the right time, rather than realizing and acknowledging their competence (Dalla-Camina, 2018)[xxii].

What are self-limiting beliefs and how do we overcome them?

Overcoming something that's embedded in our mind

and soul is never easy but when something is holding you back, you have to start to think about 'why'. Self-limiting beliefs are when we assume or believe something, and it prevents us or limits us from doing something else or moving on with our life. This is a tricky thing to spot and we don't always know why we feel or think the way we do, so *how do you detect your self-limiting beliefs?*

To detect your self-limiting beliefs, you need to question your own behavior and ask why you react in a particular way. Try reflecting on a time you really wanted to do something, but you didn't do it, because something held you back. This could be something like singing at a karaoke in public or speaking to a group of people at a meeting. *What stopped you? Why didn't you do it?* A great way to work on this is to actually reflect on your journal and question yourself. This will help you to get to the heart of your beliefs. Someone who didn't sing at a karaoke, may believe they are a bad singer, and nobody will like their singing. But remember, plenty of people who are not experts in singing, sing at a karaoke for fun. It's not a serious activity, it's a social and fun activity. By recognizing this belief, you can start to make changes.

Once you can detect your own self-limiting beliefs, you can start to think about how you can push past your belief and make a new one. For example, if we refer to the karaoke example, a person may decide that they take the idea of sing at a karaoke too seriously. If they really want to sing at a karaoke, then they should do it. You can make a plan to move past this, so next time you have an opportunity to sing at a karaoke, you are going to do it because it is a fun activity and not a serious activity. You may start to tell yourself it doesn't matter whether or not you can sing.

Making a plan to alter your beliefs and overcome your fears can be a really refreshing experience and this helps you to push past limits. Planning ahead motivates you and once you've overcome the fear, you are no longer limited as you feel a sense of freedom. Start small at first, so that you don't overwhelm yourself. For example, sing with a friend or in a group if you are still too scared to sing alone, and then build up to singing alone.

How can I start to trust myself and instill self-belief?

If you have some automatic thoughts that stir-up self-doubt, you often don't even realize it's happening. Such negativity brings you down but when we automatically think in a specific way, it becomes nature to us.

Building up trust and self-belief is something we must work on as it doesn't come easy. *So, how do you start to do this?* First of all, you need to detect and unpack our beliefs as we discussed in the earlier sections. This is important because the first step is to understand ourselves and our beliefs.

Once you know and understand your beliefs, you need to make new ones. If we think of the karaoke example again, we need to change the fear of what other people think of our singing, to the idea that singing at a karaoke isn't serious singing anyway, it's just a thing to do for fun. As long as you have fun, the singing doesn't matter. Transform your beliefs into new ones and write them down. Detail them as being **my new core beliefs** and look at them every day. Writing them down is an important step because when you write something down, it's there, it's serious, and we think about it differently because we have essentially made a written contract with yourself.

The next step is to accept where you are now. Acceptance is important when you're trying to build up trust, because only then can you be honest with yourself. Think about where you are now and where you want to be.

You can then start to talk yourself into believing in yourself again. Yes, you did just read that correctly - you can talk yourself into believing in yourself. We've already talked previously about affirmations. They can be used to reprogram the mind and we can start to believe in ourselves again. Use your newly formed beliefs to shape everything you do from now on.

To move on further, you really need to start on getting rid of those negative thoughts and feelings, but this takes some time and work. Start by noting down any negative thoughts you have and then answer them with a positive thought. This is something you can do continuously and build on over time. Eventually, you'll start to refrain from negative thoughts and automatically think positively.

Set for yourself a new challenge. We fall into certain behavior patterns and when we stop trusting or believing in ourselves, we stop taking on challenges and learning new things. Start by setting a small challenge for yourself, push yourself to succeed in that challenge and you can see your confidence, trust and self-belief begin to grow.

Don't compare yourself to others. This again links to acceptance as you need to accept that you are you! We all like different things, and we all appear and sound differently, yet we feel the need to be someone else. Be yourself, accept yourself, and only ever try to improve yourself. You will always fail at being someone else because you are best at being you.

Set your own boundaries. When people lose belief and

trust in themselves, they start to do things they don't need or want to do because they feel obliged to. It's important that you set boundaries. Think about what you are and are not prepared to do. Fear often stops us from saying no and setting boundaries, but this is not a bad thing. A person who sets boundaries shows great leadership and assertiveness skills and this often builds a respectful culture. Ensure that you set both internal and external boundaries!

Self-doubt versus living with solid self-trust

While a certain amount of self-doubt is normal, it is important not to lose sight of what this can lead to. If your feelings and thoughts spiral out of control and you become anxious. This means it can become increasingly difficult to reel yourself back in as trust takes time to rebuild.

There is no question that too much self-doubt can lead to misery as we can end up living our life around it when we allow fear to take control of our life. If we trust ourselves, we take calculated risks and we are much happier. We are more likely to overcome barriers than simply being stopped, because we are programmed not to accept that. We can learn to see our barriers as a challenge rather than giving up and because we trust ourselves, we grow and develop as people.

When someone doesn't trust themselves, they stop controlling their own life. For instance, they lose accountability and blame others when things go wrong. A person who does not trust actually gives very little back to society. It's not necessarily their own fault, but their lack of trust stops them from contributing effectively as they distance themselves and shirk responsibilities.

People who trust themselves are open to improvements, have a strong sense of accountability, and they are ready for self-development and growth. They are influential figures because they make a difference and become well-respected. Imagine you're in the workplace and you're not sure how to handle a particular complaint by a customer. You know that the business gets a lot of work from this particular customer. *So, who do you go to?* Of course, you would go to the person who had made themselves a strong figure in the workplace – this is an important customer and you wouldn't hand them over to anyone. It has to be the most competent person who trusts themself and has your respect. You know that they will do their utmost to ensure that the issue is resolved and has little impact on the business as the customer will be looked after.

For a person who has a strong sense of self-trust, their confidence is more likely to improve too, because they begin to know what they want and become determined to get it. They treat themselves with the respect they deserve and by doing so, they demand it from others. We all deserve this, and we just have to find our pathway to building, developing and nurturing this trust.

Day 10-12 of your 30-day Recovery Plan

JOURNALING

How is your journaling going? Are you doing this every day? Journaling is great for capturing information, emptying our head and it's also useful if we just need to let off some steam. We've spent so much time focusing on behaviors, thought patterns and feelings, and let's face it, those things can become overwhelming.

Backtrack over the last three-five days and read your journal. At the end of each day, I want you to think about something positive – something you are proud of maybe. It doesn't have to be long but make a little note to remind you of this positive thing.

ACTIONABLE STEP

Take part in something that you would normally avoid. For example, if you usually avoid speaking at a team meeting, offer a five-minute talk. Note down the thoughts you have before and after. Think about how the experience has enriched you. It's fine to think about what you would do better, but also think about what you did well too.

ACTIVITY

1. Write a profile/description of a person you would trust. What would they do to gain your trust? How would they behave? What are their ethics? What type of person are they? This person is a reflection of you and your ethics. Are there any reasons why you shouldn't trust yourself? Remind yourself that you can trust yourself by keeping this description to hand.
2. Set yourself a challenge. Think of something that you really want to do, but for some reason, you haven't done it yet as a result of self-doubt.
3. Write some objectives – what do you need to do, to achieve this?
4. This is your first challenge, so don't overwhelm yourself but make it worthwhile. It has to be something that you really want to achieve in order to make sure you feel motivated.
5. Reflect on your achievements for the week. Write down your biggest win and share it with a friend or family member.

Chapter 5

Soothe Anxiety and Learn to "Recharge" Your Confidence

What do you think of when you hear the word soothe? For most people it means calm and ease. *What about the word, recharge?* For me, this is reviving something or bringing it back to life. Sometimes we need a confidence boost or recharge because maintaining confidence requires a lot of energy. It's like your cell phone, you can keep going for a long time, but eventually, your battery needs a rest and boost.

Soothing our anxiety and confidence is a skill we can learn ourselves. Think about when a baby is soothed. It's taken into a calming environment and pacified in some way until the baby is no longer twisting or crying. In order to soothe our anxieties, we need to feel calm and nurtured, but in order to do this we need to find out more about ourselves, explore our triggers and consider the actions that ease our thoughts and feelings. You should also be thinking about self-care as it's important to take care of both your body and mind, if you want to make progress. Learning to manage and boost our anxiety and confidence leads us on our journey to self-improvement.

How symptoms of anxiety could be knocking your confidence

If we suffer from anxiety, we are suffering an array of physical, mental and emotional symptoms. *Is it surprising to hear that this may be knocking your confidence?* Anxiety is when we become consumed by those feelings and reactions, and rather than controlling them, we allow them to control us. This is why anxiety and self-confidence are so closely related, because both can take over.

If we feel anxious, we have all sorts of irrational thoughts. We can start to avoid social situations and we can even have trouble sleeping even though you feel fatigued. Avoiding social gatherings and feelings of tiredness can start to knock our confidence. We might not feel like we are at our best and this can start to impact us as we don't feel good about ourselves. In addition, we could start to have other symptoms like panic attacks; we could struggle to concentrate, be irritable, agitated, and constantly feel worried. When we have such feelings, our brain is so occupied with the negatives that we stop caring for ourselves.

As soon as we stop caring for ourselves, we are in danger of heading on a downward spiral. We know we're not at our best. If we are exhausted, we may not look our best and we could struggle to concentrate. If we can't concentrate, we may not do our job to the best of our ability. It's not long before those thoughts begin to flare up, and we start bringing ourselves down. *If we make a single mistake, it means we're not good enough, right?* Of course not, but this is how we feel because we become irrational and we become harder on ourselves. It's emotionally and physically exhausting!

We don't always notice anxiety when it first starts to happen. That's because it often happens in a gradual way. As mentioned earlier, it makes us react in an irrational way; a way we can't explain at first. We can't help reacting in that specific way even though we know it's wrong. We could be super-emotional, extremely nervous, fidgeting, feel ill or sick in particular, or we could simply feel tense, restless, or panicked. Symptoms of anxiety are different for everyone and this makes it difficult to spot initially. Mindsets can change and sufferers can have a sense of danger occurring, or impending doom. Eventually the anxiety takes hold and it starts to control everything you do.

Some people suffer from a change in their breathing when they are anxious, or they sweat, and their heart rate increases. With these particular symptoms, many people find breathing into a paper bag useful, as it helps to regulate breathing and calm the nerves.

Confidence and anxiety are very closely linked. Imagine the symptoms discussed above – *can you imagine a person that suffers such terrible symptoms being able to portray themselves as being confident?* A person who feels anxious can damage their confidence, but a person who lacks confidence can also make themselves anxious too. They are both emotional reactions that are often fed by fear and both are completely normal, providing they do not spiral (Healthline, n.d.)[xxiii]. It's extremely important to work on confidence and anxiety too and recognize the signs at an early stage.

Both confidence and anxiety issues can actually be brought under control relatively easily in most cases, by making healthy choices and by spending some time working on ourselves, *but what happens if they spiral out of control before we take action? So, if we're overloaded or feel anxious, what can we do to recharge our confidence and keep those feelings of anxiousness at bay?*

Effective rest and stress-relief strategies that help you control your anxieties

If you're struggling with anxieties and stress now, and you feel they are starting to beat down your confidence, it's important to take action. For some reason, many of us are more of the 'suffer in silence' type, but that doesn't help anyone. If we need help or guidance, we can only get this if we admit we need assistance. *Good news!* There are some things you can do if you want to control your feelings and actions:

- Change how you think. This isn't as easy as it sounds but if you are a negative thinker, you really need to start changing how you think. Make a conscious decision to change this and spend time working on yourself. Set goals and think about how you want to improve and what you want or need from life.
- Find something that comforts you. We all have our home comforts or comfort zone, so think about what yours is. Now, we should never use our comfort zone to hide, but we can use it to rest and recharge. There's nothing wrong with taking a day off!
- Don't try to leap, take small steps. Any progress is

better than no progress, but it's important to focus on your goals. Nothing is going to transform you suddenly into a confident person, but you can make improvements and progress.

- Get plenty of rest. *How can anyone be expected to feel good if they don't take care and rest themselves?* Rest is so important to keep us healthy in both mind and body, so make sure you take your rest and get enough sleep as needed.
- We can boost our confidence and improve our anxiety by treating yourself. Have a facial, take a long soak in the tub, get your hair done, or do something else for yourself (treats in the home can be just as good). This can make us feel good or better, as personal hygiene and little treats can really improve our state of mind, and in turn, our motivation. It is also a great way to relieve stress.
- Accept your mistakes and don't hold onto the past. Remember that as a human being, we all make mistakes and use them to learn. Embrace them. Appreciate everything around you and live for the moment. Don't just accept mistakes, accept your past too, but live in and for the present. No regrets!

- Create a calming environment. Create a place you can relax and will feel comfortable and ensure you're away from things like coffee or loud music. You may wish to light candles, burn incense sticks or essential oils. You can rest, put up your feet and breathe deeply, while listening to calming music.
- Define what you want in life, make plans and don't give up. How will you achieve it? How will you get what you want? It's good to have plans and direction in your life, and a person who knows what they want is often more confident.
- Make healthy choices. Make sure you eat healthy snacks and stay hydrated. Things like fruit are ideal, and you should definitely drink plenty of water to help you stay hydrated. You could also try some yoga stretches too, as this is a very relaxing and soothing exercise that can help to clear your thoughts.
- Do something you don't usually do – something different or even a little spontaneous. Everyone likes a little bit of excitement in their life from time to time and this can really recharge and boost your confidence (Lifehack, n.d.)[xxiv].

How can resting and taking care of myself help my confidence?

Some of the ways to rest and refresh are so simple and yet so effective, but by now you'll be wondering how such things can help improve confidence and we may refer back to that word again... *Soothe*.

When we feel anxious or stressed, we can't possibly think straight. Our brain skims through our thoughts and feelings at a faster rate, and it becomes difficult to process information. This can lead to burn out, which means we feel drained of our energy. We are far from our best and this can increase the intensity of our anxiety and stress because when we are not feeling at our best, we make mistakes, we don't perform well, and we put extra pressure on ourselves because of this.

If we suffer from anxiety, we need to soothe the feelings that surround it. It's no good telling someone to 'get on with it' as this doesn't help. Someone with anxieties need to feel a sense of calm, they may need to be nurtured, and most importantly, they need to feel safe.

You can actually soothe your anxieties by resting and taking care of yourself, but we'll discuss this further, later.

If you don't get help, you will eventually hit burn out. This is because your anxieties will get worse if they aren't soothed. When someone hits burn out, it can take much longer to recover, so it's best to prevent getting to that stage. Our bodies and minds tire, as anxieties tend to drain our energy. It's so important to rest well in order to function efficiently. When we are well-rested, feeling good and thinking straight, it helps us to feel confident and happy.

Many people talk about resting to recharge their batteries, but it is possible to also recharge your confidence with rest, and a little positivity. Being in a peaceful environment can calm the mind and your confidence will improve as the mind clears of its thoughts. If you struggle to rest well, try deep breathing or meditation.

For example, let's think about meditating…

By meditating daily, we can rest our whole body. We can also follow guided meditations that help us focus on the positive things, avoid anxiety and improve our mindset and the way we are thinking.

Ultimately, resting gives you the energy boost you need to carry on with your life, drive forward and work on your confidence. You can introduce many things into your daily routine that will boost your energy and in turn, your confidence.

Your resting needs to be quality. You need somewhere peaceful that you can kick back and relax, even close your eyes. Being away from false light and in a quiet environment can also help. Rest doesn't necessarily mean sleep, but sleep is important, so ensure you get enough sleep through the night. Maybe you just need a quick nap to recharge and that's fine too!

How can I make changes to boost my energy levels?

There's nothing worse than having low energy. It can

affect mood, motivation and even concentration. Having good levels of energy can really help to boost your confidence and this can generally make you feel better. There are some things you can do to boost your energy levels and seven of those are listed below.

1. Having a routine that includes rest and sleep time can improve your health and wellbeing, which will certainly boost your energy. Yes, we've already mentioned sleep but it's so important. We'll cover routines in the later chapters.
2. You should also have breakfast and keep well hydrated, by drinking plenty of water. Again, we've covered water but again, this is vital.
3. If you struggle to switch off in the evening, you should use your journal to empty your mind and just write down whatever is in your head so you can deal with this the next day.
4. Exercising first thing in the morning is also a proven method to help you boost your energy levels. A brisk walk first thing can be a great way to set yourself up for the day and boost your energy.

5. Many people enjoy making more mindful changes, like meditation and breathing exercises. Reflecting in your journal and on your day can also be really valuable, especially if you focus on the positives.
6. You can also use affirmations to positively reinforce each day. Write them out on a post-it note and stick them somewhere you can review them every day.
7. Other people enjoy reading or writing too, as this is a great way to relax and recharge. Read something you can really get into and write whatever is on your mind.

If you make small lifestyle changes like the seven listed above, you will notice a difference to your energy levels almost instantly. Boosting energy levels can be really effective and when we feel energized, it generally makes us feel happier. You should consider making small changes as smaller changes are more effective than larger changes and they are more likely to be successful.

Take small steps because each step is long-lasting progress that you can be proud of Approach these changes with an open mind and give each one a try.

You have nothing to lose!

Day 13 – 15 of your 30-Day Recovery Plan

JOURNALING

Do you journal in the morning or evening?

When you journal in the evening, you can empty your head before bed, reflect on your day, make plans for tomorrow or further into the future, and consider things you have learned or have made you happy. It's a chance to empty your head and often people who journal in the evening, sleep better. Some people prefer to do this the next morning, when they have had more time to digest the information and that can work too, but remember that the mind isn't always fully awake when you first wake up, so you may need to wait until you've got dressed and had some breakfast before you begin.

Don't forget to keep journaling and ensure you spend some time reflecting on your days and experiences!

ACTIONABLE STEP

In this chapter we've looked at confidence, and we've also focused on taking chances, reducing anxiety and boosting your energy levels.

You have 3 actionable steps for each day, to help you boost your energy levels:

1. Plan a new routine that includes staying hydrated and exercise first thing.
2. Arrange a social event with friends.
3. Visit Youtube and try out a guided meditation that focuses on positivity, confidence or success.

If you want to make changes, it's important to take positive action.

ACTIVITY

Your activity in this chapter is to try free writing and this requires some level of commitment from you. This is different to journaling, because you can write anything, but you don't have to think (in fact it's better if you don't), and it doesn't have to be structured. It's a great way to spark your creativity:

- When you go to bed in the evening, leave a notepad and pen next to your bed.
- Set your alarm 30 minutes earlier than usual (sorry, but this part is crucial. You can do it).
- As soon as your alarm bell rings, pick up your pad and start writing whatever you feel like writing. Remember this is free writing, and you shouldn't think, just write anything that springs to mind. You can make sense of all later, as the idea is that you're writing without being fully awake, so it's from your subconscious.
- Write for between 10-20 minutes.
- Try 5 minutes of meditation afterwards and do some Yoga stretches if possible.
- Once you're dressed and have had breakfast, go back to your writing and read what you've written. *Does anything catch your eye?* You may be able to use some of this for various reasons – for creative purposes or as a to-do list / reminder.

Free writing is great for creative people as it can really encourage your creative spark. Some people have stressed that they aren't creative people, but then they flourish in this exercise. Give it a try! Being creative could mean you're creative in your ideas or in business, so don't assume it has to be arts, crafts or writing. Being creative is so much more, it's an expansion of our ideas and it's something that we are all capable of. Don't sell yourself short until you've tried it – you may even be surprised!

Chapter 6

Check Your Self-Image to Eliminate Tendencies of Comparison

How do you feel about your own image? Are you happy with it? You'll be surprised how many people say *no!* It's human nature to form opinions, we do this automatically. When we open a magazine or watch the television, we may wish we had hair like the lady on the shampoo advert or are hope that we are as thin as a certain movie star. That's because we have the consistent need to compare ourselves to others or wish for those things we don't have.

If we keep focusing on what we don't have, it's hard to remain positive and happy. It's just as important to focus on what we *do* have. The way we feel about ourselves, and our need to compare ourselves can become unhealthy. It's certainly bad for our state of mind. If a person isn't happy with their self-image, then they should change it. But you need to concentrate on being more like *'you'*, not in the image of someone else.

What do we mean by 'self', what is self-image, and how is it formed and developed?

The word self ultimately refers to us. It's our opinion of who we are and what we look like. The idea of 'self' is talking or thinking about our own self. We all have opinions and ideas of our self, as we know who we are and what we're about... *Or do we?* Although it's normal to form an opinion of our self, we are known to be harsh. Sometimes, we aren't necessarily positive and while we might think highly of ourselves at a certain point of our life, this doesn't mean we'll always feel like that. As humans we have high and low points throughout our life.

What we think of ourselves, isn't necessarily a reflection of what others think as we are programmed to criticize ourselves. When we suffer from confidence issues, it can be really difficult to see the positives, especially when referring to our self. While we may think we are weak in nature, others may see us as being strong and independent. Perception is everything when it comes to referring to one's self. That brings us nicely onto self-image, because what we see in the mirror isn't necessarily what someone thinks. We may not like one of our facial features, like our nose, but others may think it suits our face. A person with an eating disorder may see someone as overweight when in fact, other people see someone thin and struggling.

It's reasonable to suggest that our ideas of our self and self-image are formed by our own perceptions. This can depend heavily on our thoughts, beliefs, actions and emotions.

Have you ever heard anyone or even yourself say, 'I'm a mess,' when they are feeling upset? Well, we are referring to how we feel because we have been crying or at least feel like it. This reflects what we perceive on the outside too because we view the world differently when we are feeling emotional – we could feel an array of emotions, positive or negative, and each of these would influence our perception of how we feel. This may not always be apparent to other people as when we tell someone we're a mess, we might be on the inside, but to others we may look okay on the outside.

Sometimes, it is reflected in our exterior appearance. If we are fatigued, we look withdrawn and our eyes may appear sunken and have dark rings surrounding the socket. A person who we are close to may notice this, but sometimes we hide how we feel by slapping on some make-up to hide the tiredness. For some people, this boosts their confidence and they are able to portray a positive self-image. But this doesn't work for everyone!

The opinions we form when it comes to ourselves are

difficult to explain because we are individual. How we feel about our self is down to our own personal beliefs and automatic thoughts. We make assumptions, and because we are talking about us, we feel our judgments are justified. *Who knows us better than we know ourselves?* Well, that's a very good question.

In truth, we form opinions based on our beliefs, thoughts and feelings, but as these things can change and develop over time, so does our opinion of ourselves. For example, a woman in her early twenties with a good job may feel great, but she may then get married and have a child and as we head into the later twenties to early thirties, she may feel differently about herself. Maybe her career is on hold, she's not as fit or thin as she used to be, and she feels starved of the intelligent company she was a part of for so long. Those things are less important to her now, but that doesn't mean she doesn't miss them, even though she wouldn't change the path she chose. This could have a detrimental effect on how she feels about herself, but also, we can't forget the 'mom-guilt' she'll also feel right now. She became a mother and it was the best thing that ever happened to her... so *why does she crave intelligent company? Why is she bothered about her looks, weight and fitness? Her career is only on hold for now until the most precious thing in her life goes to school or grows up, so why does she feel like she's lost?*

For some women, they would instantly chastise themselves for feeling that way and brand themselves a bad mother. Yet, when we don't work or have a career, we can also be seen as a poor role model. That's right, we can't win!

The most important consideration to ask yourself here is, *what's right for me or us?* When you build your confidence, you will choose your path with ease and overcome these barriers because you will only be concerned with the greater good for you and your family, and not the judgments placed on you by society or individuals. Such things will be insignificant to you because they have no impact on your life.

Over time, those things that are important to us change,

and this alters how we feel about our self and how we view our self-image. There still could be part of us that wants that something we once had, but as we evolve, our priorities change. As we move on in our life, we experience new things and we change our beliefs. As we hit the bumps in the road on the way, things become more important while others become less. Someone who isn't bothered about their weight may find they have a health condition and suddenly, they may realize that they have to change their diet and lose weight. This will totally change the way they feel about themselves. Failing or relapsing will also cause depressive or negative thoughts and we could beat ourselves down in our mind.

While our ideas and opinions of ourselves comes from us, let's not forget that sometimes there are external factors that shape how we feel and think. We are often forced into comparing ourselves to others, but this can lead to feelings of inadequacy. By comparing ourselves, we can actually cause ourselves to feel down and depressed.

Have you ever looked in a magazine at an image of a model wearing that new lipstick you want or a swimsuit you love, but you feel inadequate because you know you can't compare to her?

Stop this, right now!

How comparing ourselves makes us unhappy and gives our confidence a bashing

Society likes to organize everything and everyone, so it's normal for us to put ourselves and everything we do into little boxes or categories. While healthy competition is normal, doing this to an extreme can be harmful because it causes us to constantly judge and compare ourselves with others. We are generally happier if we are ourselves, so it's important to just be yourself.

If you don't want to wreck your confidence and self-esteem, then you shouldn't compare yourself to others.

If we refer back to the swimsuit example in the earlier section, we already feel depressed because we know that we're never going to look like the image of the perfect model wearing it. It was made for her. The question is, *why do we want to look exactly like her?* If we all appeared the same, wore exactly the same clothes and were shaped in the same way, we would lead very boring lives.

Comparing ourselves to others makes us unhappy but it's something we do as human beings. It's a learned behavior that we pick up from a young age and it creates a disconnection between ourselves and others. It means we follow social norms in society in an attempt to fit in with others and blend in well, yet this very thing makes us feel inadequate. This is because it's not really us as we aren't being our true selves. There is always someone out there that is doing it better or looks better and this makes us feel like we are not good enough. We are much happier if we are true to our self. Although we do not necessarily learn uniqueness, it is vibrant, and it stands out. We should therefore view a confident person as being unique in a positive way, because we are taught to blend in and follow social norms, being unique is something we have to warm up to. We have to work on this.

If you want to be happy, you must change this behavior right now and stop comparing yourself to others. This will help you to rebuild and instill a new-found confidence. The word unique means to be individual and different. Someone who is unique is not like anyone else, so this is often something we must discover and become comfortable with on our own. Once we do this, our confidence can grow and thrive.

If you want to stop comparing yourself to others, there are a few things you must do:
- Remember that things aren't always what they seem. The lady in the swimsuit may have had the swimsuit fitted and her pictures airbrushed professionally. Nobody is perfect.
- Cling to your self-worth and remember that it's what's on the inside that matters. You are your own person.
- Do what's right for you! Just because others are

doing a certain thing, doesn't necessarily mean that thing is right for you, right now. Don't worry about what others are doing just focus on what you are doing and what your strengths are.
- Remember that we all have weaknesses as we can't possibly be good at everything. Give yourself a break!
- Know what you want! Think about your own interests and what you like to do. *What are you good at?*
- Be realistic. It's no good placing expectations on yourself that you are never going to achieve. Always be reasonable with your expectations.
- Always focus on the positives. It's not always easy to be positive about yourself but you should certainly focus on the good points.
- Be unique and be happy! Individuality is a positive thing so use that and embrace it.
- While it's normal to have healthy competition, remember that everything doesn't have to be. Just simply aim to be the best person you can be!
- Find out your purpose. Think about what you want in life and what matters to you.
- Enjoy yourself! Give yourself permission to enjoy

life, do what you love and take care of yourself (AGATHANGELOU, 2015)[xxv].

Self-esteem and confidence in a digital age

There are many pros and cons to social media when it comes to self-esteem and confidence. While social media can be used to post motivational quotes, affirmations, success stories and adverts that will help improve self-esteem and confidence, just like the paper-based media, there are things that can smash it too.

You might feel really bad about yourself. Maybe you don't have much money for Christmas as you're going through a difficult time, and people start posting how many presents they have got for their family or how much money they have spent, this will not make you feel good. It sends you on a spiral. Again, people can modify images and post picture-perfect lives that you can only dream to have. You need to be aware that not everything on social media is true. The lady two blocks away who bakes the most amazing cookies and appears to be the most amazing mom with the most well-behaved, clean and happy kids you've ever seen is probably not all she seems. That's because social media is filtered, and people only allow you to see what they want you to see.

Isn't it a great feeling when you finally get to see an honest post, video, or picture on social media that shows life's little imperfections? That's because it's real! Life is full of imperfections and all those posts, images and videos that make you feel inadequate are not a true reflection or representation of life.

Recent studies have shown that regular Facebook users have shown a decline in mental health, and self-esteem. A recent study considered the detrimental and negative impact this can have on our mental health. One study in particular explored patterns between different Facebook habits and found that of the many 1,104 people who participated, the ones who engaged regularly with Facebook ended up with deteriorated mental health, felt body shame and lower self-esteem (Petersen, 2017)[xxvi].

Regardless of the negative impact social media appears to have on several people, we continue to return to it and use it. *Why is that?* Well, social media has grown into a huge media platform and now everyone uses it, including businesses. You can use social media to communicate, to sell, to buy, and to advertise your products and services. Students can use it to communicate with classmates and complete study projects and you can even use social media for research purposes too. Wherever we go, we can rarely escape the clutches of social media, and that's because there are many benefits to this too.

We should, however, control our usage, take breaks as required, and change our own thoughts, beliefs and feelings when using this to enable us to remain effective and efficient when using it. We need to be aware of the effects of social media and allow ourselves to take back control, without letting it affect our self-esteem and confidence. Sometimes simply being aware that such things can cause problems can allow us to move forward.

Day 16-18 of your 30-day recovery plan

JOURNALING

Journaling plays a large part in your recovery, so hopefully you're still doing this daily. While you may have very little to write on some days, you may have lots to write on others. Don't worry, there's no right or wrong way to do this!

Just for the next three days, you should monitor your social media usage in your journal. The main point of this is to raise your awareness – don't use it more, don't use it less, just use it as you would on a typical day. For fun, before you begin, estimate how long you think you spend on social media, in one day.

Social media can really impact how we feel and sometimes, we don't even realize the affect it has over us. Over the next three days, note down the times you use social media in your journal so that you can monitor this and answer one question – *how do you feel after your social media session?*

Did you estimate how much time you spend on social media in total in one day, correctly?

ACTIONABLE STEP

In this chapter we've talked about self-image, our view of our self, and things that can lower our self-esteem and confidence, like social media.

You have 3 actionable steps for each day, to help you boost your energy levels:

1. List three things you think about your 'self' and 'self-image' Keep it positive!
2. List your strengths and three things you are proud of.
3. Write down three things you would like to change or achieve in your life.
4. Study these and write some goals that focus on how you can use your opinions of yourself and your strengths to achieve those things.

ACTIVITY

Your activity in this chapter is to explore your 'self' and self-image.

- Write a list about yourself – positive and negative.

- Look at the negative – *why do you believe those things about you? Think* about your childhood or any influences in your life. This could be your parents' beliefs, societal beliefs, social media etc…
- Look at yourself in the mirror. *What do you see?*
- Write down anything you would change.
- Now ask another person, someone you trust, *what are three positive and negative things they would say about you?*
- Ask them about your image too – *how do you look (tired, happy etc…)?*
- Analyze this and think about anything you would change. *What would you change? How?*
- Think about how your own personal beliefs impact how you view yourself and your image. *Are they irrational or rational? Realistic or unrealistic?*

Chapter 7

Uncover the Negative Stories You Tell Yourself to Rewrite Your Inner Dialogue

In the previous chapter we talked about beliefs, but most of the time, even if we don't really acknowledge it, our beliefs are based on a story. *Have you ever talked yourself out of doing something?* Say you're invited to party, but before you go, you've talked yourself into believing that you're not going to have a good time, and you don't. Then you feel a sense of satisfaction, because you were right, you didn't have a good time. You know things could've gone very differently had you been in a positive mindset and that's because we control our own stories.

Our life is made up of stories. Our stories make us who we are. Stories are based on our experiences and beliefs, as they are things that we tell ourselves within our minds, using our internal dialogue. Remember that stories aren't always the whole truth. That party you went to that was lame, but several people at that party had a good time; you had a lame time because you'd talked yourself out of wanting to go. You shaped that story, but *why did you shape that in a negative way?*

We all have a story to tell our self, but how accurate are they?

In the previous chapters we've talked about self-esteem and confidence, and how we can be harsh on ourselves. That's all still true, but until we change our beliefs, we will continue to have the same thought and behavior patterns. Our stories are often shaped by those beliefs and impacted by our experiences in life.

We do have to be wary when believing our internal stories as sometimes what we tell ourselves aren't wholly true. It's not like we intentionally lie to ourselves. The inner dialogue that tells you stories is not your friend but a replication of your self-doubt. Your internal dialogue never stops, and it narrates everything we see, hear, and experience. The problem is that your mind can manipulate the information however it wants. The information can then be adapted and filtered as it's there to comfort you and make you feel safe. For example, if a dog bit you and you subsequently became afraid of dogs, your inner dialogue isn't going to admit that. It would tell you that you just don't like dogs anymore as it wouldn't confirm the fear. If you went to visit someone with a dog, perhaps you may say that you don't really like dogs, or they don't like you. If you were feeling really defensive you might even say you're allergic to them. That's because your inner dialogue tries to soothe and protect you. This reveals that your inner voice isn't in line with reality.

Your inner voice could become harmful, especially if your confidence or self-esteem are low. It's going to be destructive and it will try to wear you down. *Is that inner voice really what you want to lead you in everything you do?* If not, it's time to change that inner voice. We need to change its reactions, responses and even its tone. We are no longer going to accept such a negative force to guide us!

We can't stop our inner dialogue, but we do have the power to make deep changes to our mind that impacts the way we think, act and feel. By simply being aware we can change how we respond to our inner voice. We can learn to quieten the voice when it's being ridiculous, persuade it to think in a different way, and remove its power. You can do this by ignoring it, filtering it and proving it wrong. You can also distract yourself from it and clear your mind, until you can think clearly. Breathing exercises and meditation can help with this (Bokhari, 2019)[xxvii].

How important are our internal stories?

Internal stories aren't all bad and there's no denying that our stories make us who we are. We can use positive stories and experiences to shape our future too. Without our stories, we could be a completely different person as we may have made different life choices. Stories are pivotal points in our life that are instrumental in how we think, feel and act today. For instance, someone who battled a mental health issue and now helps others do so, would be really passionate about their work. People would trust them because of their honesty and firsthand experience. A person who was bullied at school and completely turned their life around and now advocates for victims would again be an asset as they would be trustworthy and capable of helping others who are being bullied. They would give hope to others. A person who suffered financial difficulties such as a bankruptcy, and then developed a million dollar company would certainly be listened to in relation to financial advice because there are so many who could identify with them. Furthermore, due to that person's experience, they would feel empathy and understanding towards their audience.

You can control the stories we use to shape who we are, and you can also choose how you portray or use them. This doesn't mean we should lie, as we should always be honest, but we, need to use them in a positive way so that they can be effective. If we refer again to the bullying example, it is much more powerful to be a success and help others as a result of enduring suffering as a victim, than it is to remain a victim all of our life. Remember, people love success stories.

Our internal stories play a huge role in how confident we are or how confident we appear. We can make the change to ensure that we make the most of that. Above, we discussed success stories and if we have a story to tell that leads to success, it makes us feel good. It's a justification of why we are successful today. It shows us in a positive light and can portray us as strong people who know our own minds and made it through hardships. Our stories are important because they connect us to others, they remind us of who we are and they provide the boost we need to increase our confidence and self-esteem, because they remind us of the journey we've taken to be who we are today.

How to observe your inner dialogue and rewrite it

It's official, you're not crazy. That little voice that twitters away in your head is really there. It's your inner dialogue, telling you what to do and nagging you. But how often do you listen, or do you tell it to be quiet?

So, how do we observe our inner dialogue? When something is chattering away inside your head regularly, you get used to it. It becomes difficult to pinpoint it, so at first you will really need to listen to yourself. *What does it say?*

Your inner dialogue is going to occur every time you're faced with a decision as well, but over time you can change it, as when an emotion or action is triggered. It's a type of automatic thought that you can't prevent. Raising awareness is a huge part of this book, and that's because awareness lays the foundation for improvement. We are on a journey to improve our confidence, and that means we need to explore our feelings, actions and thoughts. Listen for your inner dialogue.

Sometimes, our inner voice is not telling us anything positive. It could be telling you you're not good at something or you need to avoid that social event. This voice represents all your fears, doubts and insecurities. We need to learn to reshape this, and we need to investigate why our voice is saying negative things.

If you want to get to the bottom of this, you should log the events that initiate the automatic thoughts. Write down what happened, what your voice was telling you, and why you reacted in such a way. Ask yourself why your mind is telling you to react in such a way.

Negative automatic thoughts are unhealthy for us. If we are constantly replaying scenarios, beating ourselves up or thinking about mistakes, we will knock our own confidence and self-esteem for sure. This means it's imperative to question our thoughts, feelings and actions. If you're reacting, or have just reacted negatively, it's important to clear your mind before you move any further. You can relax, take a bath, read a book, exercise, take a walk, or meditate. Once your mind is clear, you're ready to begin to take action.

Take a look at the events you've noted down and ask how you would like to react. Also think about how you can overcome those negative feelings. *What can you do to prevent feeling, reacting or thinking this? What would soothe your inner voice?*

Think about what is causing you to think this way. Reflect on the pivotal points and stories in your life that shape who you are. *What belief is responsible for how you think/feel/act right now?* Once you've worked this out, you can rewrite your story in the essence it was intended. You can change it around and flip it into something positive. Form your new beliefs based on your new story. Start to harness your internal complimenting voice. This is the voice that observes the positive things you do. You also need to think about what motivates you, from within. If your internal voice was talking to you, what would it say to motivate you?

Develop an internal tone and be firm. Remember when you were a child and how mom talked to you? She used different tones, right? We have the upset tone, the disappointed tone, the happy and excited tone, the angry tone, etc... Develop your own tone inside your head. Be firm with yourself and assertive when you have to give yourself a good talking to and be upbeat when it's time to motivate yourself. If you're using those tones inside your head, you can channel them to achieve the desired effect.

Remember, internal dialogue is powerful, and it belongs to us – those are our words. We can rewrite it and use it to forge and strengthen confidence and self-esteem by challenging our stories and revising our beliefs. When you make changes to your thoughts, feelings and actions you really begin to make your confidence flourish.

To rewrite your internal dialogue, you need to question it. We don't live our lives based on the opinions of others, but we do need to accept that sometimes, we won't agree with what our internal voice says. If someone tells us that we can lose weight if we follow a certain diet, we want proof. With that in mind, we should never take our internal voice at face value, because it's only worth listening to if it's making valid points. When your voice starts chatting on, make sure it's being relevant, and its claims are founded. If not, you need to hush it up – be stern. *Is it a justified point? Is it constructive or argumentative? Does your voice have any evidence that backs up its claim?* In order to rewrite your internal dialogue, you need to be able to quieten it down before it gains momentum. If your inner voice talks to you in a negative way, remind it that it needs to be positive. In time, your voice will learn to react in a productive way that is of benefit to you, rather than hindering.

Day 19-21 of your 30-day Recovery Plan

JOURNALING

You've now had 18 previous days to journal. If you're struggling with ideas of what to write, really concentrate on the decisions you've made. Think about what led you to that decision.

REFLECTION: Look at your journal for the last three days and consider anything that you've done that triggered negative thoughts.

Think about your belief system – why did you react in a negative way?

Think about your ideal – how would you like to react?

Think about your story – what story from your past impacted the way you reacted?

ACTIONABLE STEP

Rewrite a pivotal story in your life. A pivotal story is something that changed your life and you've altered what you do or how you think ever since. It's a turning point. For example, a woman could have a child, and suddenly find that they develop stronger career aspirations and may want to change their job, progress or even go back to education so that they can make a better life. Having a child made her want more and aspire to be more.

Our lives are full of pivotal stories that shaped the path we have taken so far. Sometimes we do things because of the way we've been treated, to prove somebody or ourselves wrong, or because of an event that has occurred and either inspired or motivated us. If something happens that has pushed us into action, then it's a pivotal story.

What're your pivotal stories?
1. Think of three stories that have influenced your life. They must include a pivotal point. They can be positive or negative and you should ask yourself, what did I learn?
2. Reflect on the goals you wrote in the previous chapter.
3. Rewrite your stories based on what you've learned or achieved and consider how you can use them to shape your future and achieve your goals.

ACTIVITY

Your activity in this chapter is to challenge your beliefs and internal voice.
- Write down your core beliefs. If you aren't sure what your beliefs are, reflect on your journal and pinpoint how your beliefs or life events contribute to the way we view things. Think about why you believe that/think that/feel that/react like that and then you

will begin to unpack your beliefs.
- Write down your belief, and if it's negative, challenge it. For example, if you come from a poor background, you may think that you are destined to never make money. You need to flip that around – *who says you can't make money? Who says you can't be rich/confident/happy?* You will find that a lot of your beliefs are unfounded.
- Once you've done this, devise a list of your new core beliefs in life.
- Now you have your beliefs, use them to challenge your inner voice. If your inner voice says anything negative; anything that doesn't resonate with your core beliefs, challenge it. From now on, your core beliefs shape you, your beliefs, and your stories.

A confident person has strong core beliefs that they live by and their stories make them who they are, based on these values. It takes some getting used to, but congratulations, because once you have, you've made important progress towards improving your confidence and self-esteem.

Chapter 8

Build Self-Care Routines that Remind You of Your Worth

We often tell our friends or relatives that they should take care of themselves. This is something that you've probably been told yourself too from time to time, or maybe more often. When you're stressed or feel low, it becomes increasingly difficult to think about yourself. We may feel we don't have time to take a walk, spend a little extra time relaxing in the tub, or maybe we don't have the time or money to go to the salon or spa. In truth, we're the first people to warn others to take care of themselves and yet many people are not used to practicing what they preach. If you want to build your confidence and the feeling of self-worth, you need to change that and building a self-care routine is a step in the right direction!

Self-care and why we need it

There's been some hype surrounding the idea of self-care over the last few years. There are many coaches, counsellors, doctors, other health care professionals and even workplaces that focus on supporting or encouraging individuals to look after or care for themselves. When we have busy lives – maybe we work, run a business, have children, care for an elderly relative or are studying, and we pour our heart and soul into it, this often comes at a cost. The cost of neglecting yourself because we switch into a machine mode, and we seem to sacrifice self-care. This could mean that we become run down, depressed, less efficient, or even sick as a result. Spending some time caring for ourselves can prevent this!

Self-care obviously means to care for one's self. Sometimes we don't look after ourselves as we should, but ask yourself, *if we don't look after ourselves, who will? Who better to know exactly what we need, than us?* We are the best people to care for ourselves because we know exactly what we need to heal, regroup and refocus.

We can look after ourselves by getting enough sleep, drinking plenty of water, meditating, eating nutritious and healthy food, exercising and by treating ourselves to occasional treats like a facial or a visit to the salon, to help us feel good or relaxed. *But why is this so difficult?*

For most of us, it's in our nature to put others first and ourselves last. This is not a negative trait of ours, however, this can lead on a path to self-neglect. When we don't have a lot of time, we neglect ourselves further and then we stop listening to our own needs and kind of block them out. This also becomes natural to us because it's easy to get into the habit of ignoring ourselves. This again links back to the idea of self-worth, because indirectly, the care of ourselves is always something that we feel justified to sacrifice, above all else.

It's really important that we take care of ourselves and stop neglecting the need for self-care because there are so many benefits. We are often more productive, motivated, and happy when we care for ourselves, so not caring for ourselves is counterproductive. If we care for ourselves, we tend to be more focused and it gives us that valuable reflection time to listen to our mind. That way, we know what we want in life.

Let's also remember that self-care can also help us to keep our body and mind healthy. This can help to improve our confidence and you will soon start to realize your own self-worth.

That little voice inside of us that whispers to us whether we deserve something or not, often tells us we shouldn't spend time, energy, or money on ourselves.

We don't deserve or need it, but this is wrong. We do! We have already considered the benefits of self-care, but we do actually need it to function effectively. Self-care can fuel so many other positive changes in our life. It's the foundation for us to grow. It's time to let go of everything that bogs us down by showing ourselves a little bit of appreciation.

Many people wonder how they can possibly fit in self-care, but self-care doesn't have to be too time consuming. You can spend an extra ten minutes in the tub relaxing, give yourself a homemade facial or meditate for five-ten minutes each day. The easiest and most effective way is to build it into your schedule. You schedule in work time and other activities, so reap the benefits and schedule in self-care.

You won't be disappointed!

How to boost your self-worth

Self-worth is how you value yourself and this is something that many people generally struggle with.

We get so used to putting ourselves last and this prevents us from valuing ourselves as we don't really think about the things that we're good at.

If we're honest, as human beings we often focus on the negative things that happen rather than the positive. This isn't good for our mind and body, and we have to learn to reframe our thoughts to think of the positive things: *what do we do well? What are we good at? What good things happened?*

How can we do this?

Thoughts are automatically formed in our mind, so it isn't always easy to change our thought patterns, but awareness is the first step. If you aware of those negative thoughts that are punishing your self-worth, then you are taking the first step towards your transformation.

People often judge themselves on their net worth, appearance, social circles, career, and achievements, but these are false, and if we simply judge ourselves on these things, we are setting ourselves up for failure. These things do not necessarily decide whether or not we're a worthy person or determines how valuable we are. It's time to take a step back and evaluate ourselves on a higher level, and we must ensure we don't get caught up worrying about how many friends or followers someone has on social media. Although this could indicate popularity, this does not indicated value or worth.

When evaluating your self-worth, you should be thinking about the things that matter most and the qualities that truly define you as a person as they can boost how you feel about yourself. Think about happiness, positivity, compassion, kindness, respect, and other personality traits that make you who you are. You should also think about identifying your voice and how we control this. We've talked about our inner voice and how it's great at telling us the negative things, but it needs to be managed in an effective way. Whenever your voice starts twittering on, pause it, question it, tell it to shut up. You should then remind yourself why this is false and just how valuable you are. Then you can move on.

Don't forget that you are not defined by the people who love you, it's the love we feel for ourselves. If we do value our very being, we will feel better, and typically we'll have better relationships too. Caring for others and being cared for is important for our emotional wellbeing (Ackerman, 2019)[xxviii].

Feeling well-cared for versus feeling worthy

We all like feeling loved and cared for. We allow the love and praise from others take make us feel good and encourage us, but this simply isn't enough. Regardless of the relationships we have, we should still feel good and be able to stand on our own feet. It's so important to be able to encourage ourselves and we must remember that other people do not define who *we* are.

If we allow the love of others to define us, we are putting our lives in their hands and this is a mistake. It can actually damage relationships because in truth, if we don't have love and respect for ourselves, we will never have love and respect for anyone else. A healthy sense of self-worth will help you to maintain a healthy, mutual relationship with others and this love will be satisfying and stable. Of course, we do love people and if anything happens, it can make us feel low. We may even feel like part of us is missing and this is normal, but we must have boundaries.

To have an equal relationship, both parties must feel worthy and have both respect and love for themselves. In order for a relationship to be happy and survive, both people must feel self-worth. If only one person has little self-worth, it can be very draining on the other person. The person who has self-worth can help to the lift the spirits of the person without self-worth, but this can only ever be a temporary fix, because we can only lift another person's self-worth for so long as it's draining. If we have to maintain both our own self-worth and another's, it can make us feel low as we spend so much time and energy on the other person. If neither have self-worth, it can be an unhappy or sometimes destructive relationship.

If both parties feel a strong sense of self-worth, they will have a mutual love and respect for one another. When you feel appreciation for yourself, it's easier to feel appreciation for each other. This is what a healthy relationship is all about. Together, they will bring happiness and warmth. Even at times if one is a little low, they can boost each other but this is equal – one does not drain the other.

Being cared for is still important and it's kind of a basic need of human nature, it just shouldn't be the only thing that boosts us. Others are attracted to us if we are positive and confident on our own, but others can also help us to be even better.

The ability to show up confidently in your life comes from within, from this self-worth and you can do this by:
- Stop comparing yourself to others.
- Ensuring you feel self-love and respect, without relying on relationships.
- Considering your own true value based on things that are important to you or the things that matter.
- Reflecting, organizing, and reframing your thoughts.

- Spending time resting your mind and body (getting enough sleep or meditating for example).

Doing these things can send you on the right path and help you turn up confident and focused, daily (Ackerman, 2019)[xxix].

Are hobbies a type of self-care?

This question is down to your discretion and your personal idea of self-care. Many people stop their hobbies when they feel down or under pressure because they feel like they don't have the time. This is one of the worst things we can do, because if we stop doing the things we like, we end up feeling worse and we're setting on a downward spiral. Now we've talked about self-care already, and many people wonder whether doing some activities that they enjoy or are good at would pass as self-care. It absolutely does!

It's easy to lose sight of ourselves, and if we stop doing those activities we love or enjoy, it's often because our confidence is dipping. That's exactly why it's important to do those things we love and enjoy. Doing these things makes us happy, and happiness makes us feel good. This is when we are at our best and are more likely to feel confident.

If you enjoy something like swimming, crafts, or reading then you should do it, because being happy is good for your soul and it's actually the ultimate example of self-care. It's your individual method of escape. *What better way to make ourselves happy?* It's uplifting.

Days 22-24 of your 30-day Recovery Plan

JOURNALING

You're really getting on with your journaling now and that's great. Over the next three days, you should focus on self-care. Note down any self-care activities you do and think about the ones that are the most beneficial to you. *Why?*

ACTIONABLE STEP

Choose a self-care activity for the next three days – it can be as small or as big as you like. Take a longer bath, meditate for 5 minutes, or something even more extravagant – you choose!

Then answer the questions below:
- After my self-care activity, how did I feel?
- What did I do afterwards that was productive and was I more productive than usual?

ACTIVITY

At the end of your three days, reflect on your self-care activities.
Which self-care activity is the most effective for you?
Did it make you more productive?
Which self-care activity did you enjoy the most and why?
What self-care activity would you like to try in the future?

Self-care needs to be consistent in order for it to be effective. You can reap the benefits, which includes increased productivity and clearer thinking if you take the time to do this regularly. Nobody is suggesting that you take hours out of your day, but small rewards are key.

*Finally, make a plan to incorporate self-care into your daily routine.

Chapter 9

Observe Improvements You've Made to Start Giving Yourself Credit for Progress

Have you ever said *congratulations...* to yourself?

We are terrible at giving ourselves the credit we deserve. It makes us feel awkward and we also don't want to give the impression of being over-confident. It's certainly difficult to celebrate or sometimes even acknowledge our own improvements, because we simply don't always notice. This may sound silly, but while we pay attention to the achievements of others that we care about, we don't necessarily think about ourselves and observe our own progress.

This could seem like a radical idea, but it's time to change that and move forward with your confidence building. Maybe you're cringing right now, but something as simple as small, achievable goals can be a great way to monitor and observe progress.

A mistake that many people make is setting goals that aren't possible – they list their dreams and aspirations which is great, but they need to recognize them as being a future dream or aspiration rather than being one goal. In reality, the bigger goals are possible, but they are so far away and before we get to it, we have so many other steps to take along the way.

The thing that we don't see, is that these steps are progress towards that dream, but they go unrecognized. We end up feeling demotivated when it comes to our goal because it's so far out of our reach, and we don't see the leaps we are taking towards it.

Eventually our goal becomes a pipe dream.

If goals are too big, we are in danger of setting ourselves up for failure. That's not to say we shouldn't have big dreams, but we need to understand that bigger goals take time, so this is not something that you're going to achieve quickly. The smaller the goal, the easier it is to track and monitor progress.

Big goals versus small goals

A great tip for goal setting is to start with a big goal or dream (this is when you can aim big) and keep breaking it down into smaller parts until you have short, achievable goals or steps that you can achieve quickly and monitor the progress. Further to this, you need to write down your goals and tick them off as you achieve each of them. This way, you can see what you've accomplished towards your end goal.

You may already be aware of ways to goal set and mark

off your progress, but the question here is, *do you give yourself credit for these achievements?*

Many people treat ticking off their goals as a kind of to-do list, and they fail to give themselves any credit at all. It's time to alter how you monitor and observe your goals from now on. Start checking your goals weekly and commend yourself on what you've achieved.

When we make a mistake, no matter how small, we always feel bad about it, right? Most people do, in fact they dwell on it and make it out to be worse than it is. Now, what about if you accomplish a small goal? *Do you praise yourself? Do you feel good? Do you treat yourself?*

If not, then how do you celebrate the win?

If you feel bad about making mistakes and you are hard on yourself as a result, but you don't celebrate your wins, then eventually your morale will be non-existent. *How long can you keep putting yourself down, without boosting yourself up?* You are on the path to destroying your confidence and it's not a good balance because if we scold ourselves when we make mistakes, we should be boosting ourselves when we accomplish something.

If you don't celebrate your wins then you are making a big mistake. We are quick to acknowledge our mistakes, but this is a negative action that can actually affect our motivation, so *why don't we celebrate our wins and boost our motivation instead?* We'd find that if we did celebrate our wins and boost our motivation more, we could be more productive in our life.

Again, this is down to the way we think because we just aren't used to being positive and celebrating our own success. Thinking in this way would in fact, give us power and it scares us – you can boost your own positivity and motivation by acknowledging and celebrating your wins.

But why?

It's because we feel energized by chemicals that are released in our brain that make us feel proud of ourselves. This encourages us to take further action, thus increasing our motivation. When we have something to be proud of, we shouldn't be ashamed. We should be shouting this from the rooftops…

> *"When you're different, sometimes you don't see the millions of people who accept you for what you are. All you notice is the person who doesn't."*
>
> Jodi Picoult, Change of Heart
> (Goodreads.com, 2020)[xxx].

We should also celebrate when we make a change or do something successfully. For example, if we want to start exercising each day and then we successfully exercise, it's an achievement. We've made a positive change in our life and we should certainly reinforce that. If we continue to reinforce wins and celebrate them, our motivation will soar and in turn this will have a positive impact on our self-esteem and confidence (Edblad, n.d.)[xxxi].

What if I don't know I've achieved something?

This notion may seem strange to some, but whether you believe it or not, because we don't celebrate our achievements, we don't always recognize them as being an something to celebrate. When confidence is low, it can be difficult for us to automatically consider that we've been triumphant. Writing it down makes it easier to monitor progress, but how can we prevent ourselves from just ticking it off our to-do list and that being the end of it? *How can we notice our own progress if we don't recognize it?* Well, this is something we can learn. We start by learning to recognize achievements and then we work on the progress monitoring and celebrations. Remember, one step at a time!

There's no doubt that every day, you accomplish or achieve something. This could be a personal goal, a work goal or even a relationship goal but regardless, we achieve it. When you're reflecting in your journal, start thinking about what you've achieved that day. This is your first step to raising your awareness and finding out just what you're capable of.

The most important part of celebrating a win is awareness and acknowledgement. This is the foundation of this whole action. We have to be able to clearly decide whether or not something was a win or not. If it's something that you've meant to do for some time, or something that will improve your life, or something you've achieved then it's a win. Next time you tick something off your list, or you do something successfully don't just brush it off. Ask yourself – *is this a win?* Make sure you open your mind and take the lead. Be strong in your own decisions and if it meets your needs, makes you smile or feel remotely happy then celebrate. Think about your win and tell someone. Push it to the front of your mind and embrace it. Celebrate it!

Recognizing accomplishments helps us to feel good and this increases our confidence. Knowing that we are not stagnant, and we are making progress can really push us and we'll be motivated to do more. It can help us improve our feelings, anxiety, and self-doubt, and it can even prompt us to overcome our shyness and be brave.

Becoming aware takes practice at first because we get stuck in negative thought patterns and we don't even realize that. We get consumed with the negative things and we don't see what is going well or the things you are good at. *We've already said that we should write down our wins, even if it's just in the form of a to-do list, but the important thing is to set aside some time each day to reflect on these and be proud.*

When we start to notice these things, the next step is to commend yourself. Once you start to see those wins, note down how you can commend them. Really appreciate them!

Recording your wins will help you to shift those negative thought patterns, because you will soon realize that although some negative things happen, the positives outweigh them. Once you train your brain to recognize the progress you've made, you can really start to celebrate your successes.

How should I celebrate my success?

Here, we are suggesting that successes should be celebrated, but many people don't bother because they don't really know how to celebrate their successes. We wouldn't feel it was warranted if we celebrated too much, but we owe it to ourselves to ensure we don't overlook or avoid the celebration too.

Sometimes, people who celebrate wins are told they are bragging. If a female entrepreneur had a great year and made mega bucks, then she disclosed this online, several people would say she was bragging. Yet big company brands such as Walmart, for example, who would've probably made at least 20 times more than the female entrepreneur, disclose their yearly profit each year but that's not viewed in the same way. Of course, I'm not saying that there are negative comments, but because it's a big company, they are required to announce this, so nobody would see this as bragging.

It's tricky to say how others should celebrate their wins

because everyone is different, and we all have different needs and expectations. There are many ways to celebrate success but if you don't know where to start, here are a few ideas:

- Treat yourself to something – this can be something small like a book, a bath bomb, a facial or beauty treatment for example. This fits in a little with self-care as we truly deserve this rewarding thing for ourselves. Self-care itself can be a fantastic reward.
- Tell your close friends or family – this can be rewarding, as it can uplift and inspire others too. Your friends and family are sure to be happy or excited for you.
- Write about it! Maybe you could write a blog post, write it in your journal, maybe even write a letter to a relevant magazine or newspaper. It's great to look back on your written pieces later.
- Why not have a win folder or collage on your laptop or in the form of a scrapbook? It's a great way to record wins. Take a picture and have a special folder to remind you of your wins. Imagery can really help you to capture and treasure those special moments.

Now, this isn't going to happen overnight so it's important to accept that, but eventually, your thought patterns will start to change and become more positive. As this happens, and you reflect more on your wins, you will begin to notice a difference in how you feel about yourself. Your mind will recognize the good and it will become automatic for you to celebrate and be proud, rather than overlook them. This will certainly turn you into a more positive person.

If you start to measure your levels of confidence in subtle ways while ensuring you embrace the experience, you will start to improve the way you feel and boost your confidence. If you record and celebrate your wins, the only way is up for you.

Confidence and self-esteem are closely linked to the way we think, feel and act. We are a complex commodity, and everything interlinks. Increasing confidence can change the way we appear on the outside as well as the inside, as others can often tell a confident person by the way they appear and act.

Days 25-27 of your 30-day Recovery Plan

JOURNALING

There's only 6 days left of your 30-day recovery plan and by now, journaling and using your journal in a reflective way will be becoming natural to you.

Over the next three days focus on your wins, no matter how big or small. Think about what you've achieved on each day – the thing that is most important to you and find a way to record it in your journal.

ACTIONABLE STEP

Write a list of things you've achieved in your life that you are proud of. This could be personal, educational or career-based achievements – anything that you are really proud of.

Our achievements often help to shape the person we are or who we become. So, keep this list, because this is a list of achievements that you may not have even celebrated yet. Reflect on your list and feel proud!

ACTIVITY

1. For your activity this time, write a list of the things you *want* to achieve in the future.
2. Turn them into a larger goal, then break them down into smaller goals if needed.
3. Pin them up in your office or keep them in the front of your journal or a diary. Something that you use on a daily basis.
4. Plan some time in your schedule to work on these goals.
5. Tick them off as you achieve them and don't forget to celebrate your wins!

Chapter 10

Establish Actions to Move Forward into a Life Exuding with Confidence

Building confidence isn't easy, it's certainly a tricky task. Once you've built it up, the hard part is over, but you still need to take measures to ensure you don't lose it (again). You need to lay your foundations and cement them, until confidence becomes second nature to you. You can then go forward and grow!

This chapter is more about maintenance. The idea is to

ensure you overcome anxiety, self-doubt and shyness, but once you've done this, you need to keep them under control. Setbacks are normal, so don't worry if you suffer a dip in your confidence or self-esteem. You can refer back to any part of this book at any time, to help you build and develop any aspect of your confidence once more.

You should certainly watch out for the warning signs we've discussed in the earlier chapters for identifying low-confidence, self-esteem and anxiety. Use your newly found knowledge to build up a keen awareness, meaning you can solve confidence issues before they dip or spiral. Awareness and prevention are key concepts here!

Retaining confidence, even if there are setbacks

Life is full of setbacks. We have ups and we have downs; that's the way it goes. When there are setbacks, it can be hard to stay positive because we are prevented from achieving what we want to achieve.

We've talked about the way we think throughout this book, and for this part, this is no exception because we need to change the way we think about setbacks. To do this, you need to build acceptance, work on your problem-solving techniques and prepare yourself to face your fears and push forward. Setbacks are not your enemy!

First of all, please remember that setbacks happen to everyone – there are no exceptions. Therefore, it's important not to take them personally. If we separate ourselves from the setback, it won't affect our confidence so heavily as we aren't connected to it. In order to separate ourselves from our setback, we need to think about it as a separate entity and really examine it, to find out what happened and where it went wrong – *what caused the setback?* We can then learn from our setbacks which can change the way we handle things in the future. *Don't forget to reflect on what you've learned from your experience and what you will do differently next time!*

If you suffer a setback, take a moment to reflect and

solve the problem. This is another way to maintain your confidence levels and if you choose to keep on with the journaling (which is highly recommended), you can talk about this in your journal and reflect later. Take a minute, and a few deep breaths before you begin. On occasions, there may be times when sleeping, breathing exercises, or meditation might help you put things back into perspective or aid you in your mission to problem-solve your issue. Try this, and if it helps, you know you can use this method effectively in the future.

Sometimes, setbacks are a little more complex, so to get over them you should write them down and brainstorm a series of solutions. Our mindset is the reason we allow these problems to get on top of us but there is a simple way to reframe this, so you can think about setbacks in a different way...

You should treat your setback as a challenge and find a way around it. It's simply a temporary barrier that you can overcome. If you solve or overcome your setback, your confidence will remain intact.

Another great way to retain your confidence is to reflect on your wins. In chapter 9, we looked at big wins and small wins, and how we can celebrate them. Reflecting on our recorded wins can really boost us when we feel low. It could also lead us to the answer we are looking for when dealing with setbacks.

Finally, take a break and do something for you. We've talked about self-care and about celebrating both wins and achievements, but what better way to retain our confidence than helping and treating ourselves?

Once you learn to overcome your setbacks, you will feel liberated.

Don't forget to set goals for your future too and give yourself something to look forward to!

Establish a daily routine that boosts your confidence and self-esteem

Get a routine – you must've had this preached to you a

thousand times, right? Well, people who have a routine for at least part of their day are often more organized and successful so if you don't have one already, read this section and do it!

A routine helps us to stay focused and organized. It prevents us from straying, and it can help us to follow our goals and monitor progress or performance. A routine instills confidence, because we never wonder what we should be doing, because we KNOW – it's part of our routine.

But make sure your routine works for you…

The most important thing about starting a new daily routine is to do what's best for you. There are some ideas of how you can start a positive daily routine below, but if something doesn't work for you, tweak it. We are all different and have our own individual needs and expectations. The road to boosting confidence involves taking ownership of your life and not being afraid to do what's best for you in the long-term.

Start by getting early. Getting up early can really set you up for the day but remember, it's still important that you get enough sleep too. So, this means that if you're a night owl, you need to go to bed earlier and ensure you get around 7-8 hours sleep. Sleep can vary among people, so this is just a guideline. Some need a little more, while others a little less.

You must stay hydrated. Drinking plenty of water is key, in order to keep you replenished. The first thing you do when you wake up should be to drink a glass of water and rehydrate your body. You should also plan your meals and healthy snacks for the day, to keep you energized.

When we first wake up, it takes our body a short time to adjust. When you open your eyes and you've had a drink, try sitting with a notebook for 10-20 minutes and write whatever comes into your brain – don't overthink it. We've talked through this technique already, but it can be really useful. This technique can be especially useful for creative people and some people choose to keep a notebook right by their bed and do this before they rehydrate.

There are a few activities you can do to get yourself off to a positive start. The most effective is some light exercise, so get out your yoga mat, take the dog for a walk, and even try some meditation. Even if you just exercise for 10-30 minutes, it's still something and it sets you on the right path for the day.

Before you start, write down three things you are thankful for or repeat three affirmations that you can relate to. Sometimes we need to remind ourselves of the positive things in our lives.

Use a diary or to-do list when you start your day. List down anything you must achieve that day, and some extra things that you want to achieve. Be realistic! Some people opt for time-blocking, and they block out parts of their day and dedicate them to certain things – exercise, dropping kids off at school, and, mealtimes for example. If you have something big to do, do it first, and then use the rest of the day to wind down from that, doing shorter tasks.

Make sure you set your boundaries. If you say you're going to relax and start to wind down by watching TV from 9 pm, then do it. It's also recommended that you take some time to reflect on your day. *Is there anything you could've done differently? Could you have responded more positively? How could you improve or change? What did you do that you're proud of?*

If you have trouble switching off, the best thing to do is to read something to help take your mind somewhere else or try journaling. Journaling can really help you to empty your mind and as you've wrote everything down, you know you won't forget it so you can relax. Journaling for around 30 minutes each evening is highly recommended.

As mentioned earlier, ensure you get enough sleep. Go to bed earlier and relax. Take a bath or use breathing or meditation techniques if required to help you settle down. Getting enough sleep really determines how we feel and perform the next day.

Many of the things we've discussed in our daily routine relate to us taking care of ourselves. We must keep our mind and body healthy and in order. That's because being in a routine, planning for productivity, and self-care make us happy and this reflects in how we think, act, and feel. If we can start to work on ourselves and process our thoughts in an effective, yet positive way, we can harness power.

This will certainly lead to high levels of confidence and self-esteem!

The final point to make now, is to explain the importance of not being harsh on yourself. Always be prepared to forgive yourself (as well as others). It's time to accept that we all make mistakes, it's human nature. It's the way we deal with these mistakes that matters.

7 Tips to bounce back faster when you make mistakes

Everyone makes mistakes, so the most effective thing

we can do is to attempt to move past them. If we make mistakes there are some things you can do to bounce back quickly.

- Accept that mistakes are normal. Nobody is perfect - everyone makes mistakes. Acceptance is key to overcoming the problem fast.
- Give yourself a break. Don't overly scorn yourself. Acknowledge the mistake and move on.
- Move on by addressing the mistake and reframing how we view this. Admit the mistake but reframe it. If you make a mistake, you are putting barriers in your own way. You need to overcome them – this is no different than any other problem in your daily life, so you need to see it that way. View your mistake as a challenge!
- Write down what you would've done differently.
- Brainstorm your problem/mistake. How can you fix or overcome this? Maybe you can work around this? Break it down into small steps and set goals.
- Review your achievements for the last week and commend yourself. Be happy and proud!
- Meditate to clear your mind and repeat your three affirmations or the three things you are thankful for.

This will help you to feel relaxed and think clearly.

Remember, everyone makes mistakes and the most important thing is to learn and move forward. We should never bury our head in the sand, we should try to bounce back, and fast. The quicker we bounce back, the less likely we are to damage our confidence.

Negative emotions and how to deal with them

When we suffer with negative emotions, we can allow them to take hold of our very being. We need to deal with them in an effective way before they take hold. There are five steps we can take to do handle these:

1. Awareness is the first step – we need to recognize our negative emotions and thought patterns.
2. When you have a negative emotion, write it down. Make a table so you can monitor these. Think about... *How are you feeling? What happened to cause this? What would you change?* When you start to investigate what caused the negative emotion, you will often realize that it isn't that bad,

and it's something that can be reframed or fixed.
3. Once you have begun to notice, record and monitor your negative emotions; you should start to unpack them. *Do you notice any patterns?*
4. The next step is to stop reacting. Next time you notice you are having a negative emotion, stop. Pause and don't react. Rethink it. Start to deal with your emotion before it shows.
5. Use some breathing exercises to cope with the initial emotion and calm your mind. It can calm you down quickly so that you don't have time to be hard on yourself. This will be less damaging to your self-esteem and it also helps you to think clearly too.

When we begin to experience negative emotions and behaviors it's important to recognize them before they escalate. Your journaling can help you identify them and then it's important to act. Just because you have one bad day, doesn't mean you're on the path to negativity so don't let this idea control which path you choose. You have to take the rough with the smooth and that's why it's important to be tough and build our resilience.

How to develop your resilience

Your resilience develops over time. Resilience is your strength within, and this is really important. It's that little feeling or voice inside that prevents us from giving up and encourages us to keep going until we get what we're striving for. If you are resilient, you can start to handle your mistakes more effectively and as a result, your stress levels will improve with practice, every day.

Confidence and resilience work together, hand in hand. You will find that you learn to control and manage your feelings, thoughts and actions better, which means your confidence grows. Problems will affect you less because you are able to spot them early on, rethink them, and focus on solutions rather than the issue. Your confidence will start to shape your personality and you will doubt yourself less. This means you will make faster decisions, more confidently.

Being resilient means you can cope with difficult situations well and you will become an action taker by tackling problems head on and leading by example. You will spend less time dwelling on problems or reacting in a negative way, as you just learn to cope and take action.

If you want to grow your resilience further, you need to develop a positive mindset. We mentioned earlier that we should aim to prevent our negative thought patterns once we are aware, but now it's time to push that even further by turning them into something positive.

Taking care of your mind and body will help to improve resilience and stamina. It's not only important to stay physically fit, you need to be mentally fit too. Keep working on yourself and take care of yourself. Staying hydrated and ensuring you eat healthily and maintaining a healthy diet can help too.

Maintaining your ideal level of confidence and self-esteem

We all have a certain ideal level of confidence and self-esteem so once we reach that, the work is done, *right?* **WRONG...**

We need to maintain this level and ensure we don't lose this again. Repeat after me, *I will not allow my confidence to be beat down again...*

Well done, you've made the pledge and that's a start, but *how can you maintain your confidence and self-esteem?*

- You can start by continuing with the self-care. Don't allow yourself to slip back into the pattern of not caring for yourself.
- Continue with the journaling. Journaling has been a major part of this whole book and this is something you should continue with.
- A daily routine is a great way to relieve stress and ensure you have balance in your life. This again will help you to maintain your ideal level of confidence and self-esteem.
- Keep your mind and body fit and healthy. Ensure you eat healthy and keep your energy levels up by eating healthy snacks. Drink plenty of water and it can also be a good idea to limit things like alcohol

and caffeine.

- Stay aware. Question yourself and ask yourself, *am I being negative?* If you notice those negative thoughts creeping up on you, you should examine and break down your thoughts again. Reprogram your thinking and deal with these.

Keeping a healthy level of confidence and self-esteem is crucial to your success. You want to maintain this and overcome the barriers for good that scupper your happiness and niggle away at your self-worth, anxieties, and imprison your braveness. You owe it to yourself, to never allow your confidence and self-esteem to dip to such a low level. You have your methods and your tips to grow your self-confidence and develop it, and therefore you have the tools you need to grow.

We welcome and applaud the new, positive and confident, you!

Days 28-30 of your 30-day Recovery Plan

JOURNAL

Well, you did it! It's your final 3 days of your 30-day recovery plan. *How did you find journaling? Was it helpful?*

In these final 3 days I want you to really think about maintaining confidence and self-esteem. Out of everything you tried, *what methods were the most effective when dealing with your confidence issues?* You should reflect on how your confidence has improved over the last 30 days, and *how your anxiety, shyness and self-worth has improved too!*

ACTIONABLE STEP

Map out a daily routine that suits you and stick to it for the next three days. Journal about it, then at the end of the three days, reflect on your experience. Remember this routine should meet your own needs and expectations!

ACTIVITY

Create a maintenance plan to keep your self-esteem and self-confidence intact. This should be fairly simple so it can be built into your routine.

Is there anything that improves your confidence or gives you a boost?
What's your favorite method of maintenance?

Make sure you try some new methods. Maybe you could attend a music or exercise class of some sort. Once you've built this into your routine and you're trying out the methods, reflect on them.

Are there any methods that worked or did not work for you?

Remember, you can amend your maintenance plan to suit your own needs.

Moving Forward...
Now you have completed your 30-day plan, you should

understand confidence, how it works and how it impacts our lives. Confidence is complex – it's a mindset, a feeling and so much more. Confidence can help to shape our personal lives, relationships, education and careers. It can be the deciding factor in what path we choose in life. Throughout this book you've learned about the causes of high and low confidence, and its impact. You've also been talked through ways of improving this and overcoming your barriers that affect your anxiety, self-doubt, and shyness.

Now that you know yourself, the maintenance steps should be fairly simple for you to follow. You have a plan of action and at any time you can refer back to any of the chapters and activities to control, monitor, and boost your confidence again.

Your next steps in your confidence journey are simple. The goals you created in the earlier chapters are possible, and you can strive for these now. Start to make a plan of action that details how you can achieve your goals. Remember, when you learn something new, you're not an expert in that topic instantly, so it can be overwhelming. Use the tools you've learned throughout this book to shape your mindset and overcome any barriers you face. Remember to celebrate the small wins as well as the big wins, as both are as equally important.

Your courage and honesty will take you a long way. You are capable of leading this journey on your own because you are confident, strong and fearless.

DID YOU ENJOY THIS BOOK?

We would truly appreciate if you could leave a review on Amazon. We are an independent publishing company and read each and every review!

Conclusion

There's no question that confidence is the most prominent barrier when we are trying to achieve our dreams. If we don't control it, it can control us, and once it takes hold it becomes extremely difficult to dominate it once more, and this creates a problem. If there was a confidence switch attached to our mind, then everyone would've used this at some point in their life because this is not a new concept. There are attempts to batter our confidence daily, and for some of us, we self-sabotage. That's why the 30-day recovery plan in this book is so important to help us take back control and use our confidence to our own advantage.

> *"Once we believe in ourselves, we can risk curiosity, wonder, spontaneous delight, or any experience that reveals the human spirit"*
>
> E.E. Cummings (Goodreads.com, 2020)[xxxii]

There are so many things linked to the idea of self-confidence. It links to our feelings of self-worth, self-belief, our emotions, our behavior and actions. It stems from the beliefs and ideas we hold that are embedded in us and ingrained into everything we do. While confidence can be a great thing at its height, it can also lead to a downhill struggle when it is at its lowest point. That's because the E.E. Cummings quote above is true, when we believe in ourselves, we begin to take risks because it motivates us to move forward and encourages us to develop ourselves. That's because of our confidence levels.

The aim of this book initially was to raise the readers confidence and self-esteem within 30-days, but it is so much more than that. It sends you on a journey and reminds us that everyone is different, and we move at a different pace. Not only did we examine ways to improve anxiety issues, get rid of self-doubt, and develop from shy little mice into brave and confident warriors, but the recovery plan also led us on our journey of self-discovery. It is the self-discovery that fuels this journey.

The confidence journey is complex and although the plan of this book is 30-days, you should be prepared to do further work on your confidence as some people's confidence issues run much deeper than others. Remember, confidence needs to be maintained too, so it's not something that we can fix and then it's fixed for good, it's something that we need to nurture!

Self-discovery is an important part of building self-confidence, because in order to improve or develop certain aspects of ourselves, we need to really know ourselves and that includes our triggers. Sometimes, we are forced to reflect deeper and for some people, past events are painful. The most challenging part of this plan is to work through your beliefs and reflect on what your core beliefs are and what influenced them. To understand them completely, you were asked to unpack your past. We can safely say that when we've believed with certainty in things or had certain ideas for a long period of time, it's not easy to change them. It's a working progress that challenges everything we thought we believed in, and it's often the foundations we built our values on. Everyone knows that when you mess with the foundations, the whole structure needs to be rebuilt. If you have already been working on forging new beliefs and values, you need to recognize that this is a big step that may take longer than 30-days, although if you follow this book closely, you should certainly experience improvements over this time. Don't worry about this, just take one step at a time.

This book focuses a lot on building awareness and while this concept can be so simple, it's priceless when it comes to confidence. Awareness is key as we must realize what barriers stand in the way of our future. This book looks at a range of issues that are brought to light through a lack of confidence, including relationships, careers, education, and our personal life. There's no doubt that we need to be aware of when and why our confidence is low, as well as how to boost it. While nothing can stop a confidence dip, the strategies and tools have ensured we are able to overcome it, without it spiraling out of control.

Self-care is growing in popularity and everywhere we turn, people are focusing on this lately. Self-care is important, and it is known to reduce stress levels and feelings of depression. It's also amazing how much self-care relates to everything to do with the 'self' that we have covered throughout this book. Self-care has an impact on our self-belief, self-worth, self-esteem, self-doubt and most of all, our self-confidence. The whole idea of one's 'self' and the care or nurturing we provide to our self is often the driving force of everything as it's all connected. If we do not feel self-worth, we may reduce our level of self-care, but this just increases that feeling of worthlessness, and eventually affects our self-esteem, self-belief. This can then bring down our self-belief and each of these chip away at our confidence levels. These continue to reduce until we do something to stop it or it's reduced to an all-time low. As we've uncovered throughout this book, this can lead to further stress and depression, as well as other mental health issues.

Now that you've followed the 30-day Recovery Plan your self-confidence should have improved and you should be in a routine that includes self-care and journaling, and your self-confidence should be at a nice level.

Congratulations on your achievement, you've made fantastic progress!

As you know, that's not the end, but the beginning of your journey because now the maintenance begins and now you can strive for those dreams you've always wanted to achieve but have felt unable to push for. If you keep working on your self-confidence and use the tools that you've learned in this book to overcome your anxieties, your shyness and self-doubt, the world is yours and opportunities will arise! It's time to use your confidence and grab your dreams with both hands.

Can you hear it now?

Hello, it's *your* confidence calling!

Reference List

[i] Wolfgang von Goethe, J. (2019). *Self Confidence Quotes (1298 quotes)*. [online] Goodreads.com. Available at: https://www.goodreads.com/quotes/tag/self-confidence [Accessed 27 Nov. 2019].

[ii] Goodreads.com. (2020). *Self Confidence Quotes (1311 quotes)*. [online] Available at: https://www.goodreads.com/quotes/tag/self-confidence [Accessed 13 Jan. 2020].

[iii] Segal, Peter (2003). *Anger Management.* Columbia Pictures. USA. https://en.wikipedia.org/wiki/Anger_Management_(film) [accessed 11 Jan. 2020]

[iv] Roosevelt, T. (2019). *Self Confidence Quotes (1298 quotes).* [online] Goodreads.com. Available at: https://www.goodreads.com/quotes/tag/self-confidence [Accessed 27 Nov. 2019].

[v] PositivePsychology.com. (2019). *What is Self-Confidence? + 9 Ways to Increase It [2019 Update].* [online] Available at: https://positivepsychology.com/self-confidence/ [Accessed 27

Nov. 2019].

[vi] Verywell Mind. (2020). *How Self-Actualized People Frequently Have Their Needs Met.* [online] Available at: https://www.verywellmind.com/characteristics-of-self-actualized-people-2795963 [Accessed 16 Jan. 2020].

[vii] Lifehack. (2020). *10 Warning Signs of Low Self-Esteem and a Lack of Confidence.* [online] Available at: https://www.lifehack.org/articles/communication/10-warning-signs-that-you-have-low-self-confidence.html [Accessed 20 Jan. 2020].

[viii] Mcleod, S. (2012). *Low Self Esteem | Simply Psychology.* [online] Simplypsychology.org. Available at: https://www.simplypsychology.org/self-esteem.html [Accessed 7 Dec. 2019].

[ix] Psychology Today. (2018). *5 Reasons People Have Low Self-Confidence.* [online] Available at: https://www.psychologytoday.com/us/blog/shyness-is-nice/201812/5-reasons-people-have-low-self-confidence [Accessed 9 Dec. 2019].

[x] Onoda, K., Okamoto, Y., Nakashima, K., Nittono, H., Yoshimura, S., Yamawaki, S., Yamaguchi, S. and Ura, M. (2010). *Volume 5 Issue 4 December 2010 Article Contents Abstract METHODS RESULTS DISCUSSION REFERENCES < Previous Next > pdfPDF Split ViewCite Permissions Icon Permissions Share Does low self-esteem enhance social pain? The relationship between trait self-esteem and anterior cingulate cortex activation induced by ostracism.* [online] Available at: https://academic.oup.com/scan/article/5/4/385/1623198 [Accessed 9 Dec. 2019].

[xi] Psychology Today. (2018). *5 Reasons People Have Low Self-Confidence.* [online] Available at: https://www.psychologytoday.com/us/blog/shyness-is-nice/201812/5-reasons-people-have-low-self-confidence [Accessed 9 Dec. 2019].

[xii] Counselling-directory.org.uk. (2016). *Identifying low self-esteem thoughts and behaviours.* [online] Available at:

https://www.counselling-directory.org.uk/memberarticles/identifying-low-self-esteem-thoughts-and-behaviours [Accessed 9 Dec. 2019].

[xiii] Counselling-directory.org.uk. (2016). *Identifying low self-esteem thoughts and behaviours.* [online] Available at: https://www.counselling-directory.org.uk/memberarticles/identifying-low-self-esteem-thoughts-and-behaviours [Accessed 9 Dec. 2019].

[xiv] Counselling-directory.org.uk. (2016). *Identifying low self-esteem thoughts and behaviours.* [online] Available at: https://www.counselling-directory.org.uk/memberarticles/identifying-low-self-esteem-thoughts-and-behaviours [Accessed 9 Dec. 2019].

[xv] Counselling-directory.org.uk. (2016). *Identifying low self-esteem thoughts and behaviours.* [online] Available at: https://www.counselling-directory.org.uk/memberarticles/identifying-low-self-esteem-thoughts-and-behaviours [Accessed 9 Dec. 2019].

[xvi] Counselling-directory.org.uk. (2016). *Identifying low self-esteem thoughts and behaviours.* [online] Available at: https://www.counselling-directory.org.uk/memberarticles/identifying-low-self-esteem-thoughts-and-behaviours [Accessed 9 Dec. 2019].

[xvii] Counselling-directory.org.uk. (2016). *Identifying low self-esteem thoughts and behaviours.* [online] Available at: https://www.counselling-directory.org.uk/memberarticles/identifying-low-self-esteem-thoughts-and-behaviours [Accessed 9 Dec. 2019].

[xviii] Curtin, M. (2018). *Are You Shy or Introverted? Science Says This Is the Difference Between Them.* [online] Inc.com. Available at: https://www.inc.com/melanie-curtin/are-you-shy-or-introverted-science-says-this-is-1-primary-difference.html [Accessed 12 Dec. 2019].

[xix] Introvert, Dear. (2019). *Introvert / Extrovert Test: This Simple Quiz Reveals Which One You Are.* [online] Available at: https://in-

trovertdear.com/introvert-extrovert-test-quiz/ [Accessed 15 Dec. 2019].

[xx] Goodreads.com. (2020). *Self Confidence Quotes (1311 quotes)*. [online] Available at: https://www.goodreads.com/quotes/tag/self-confidence [Accessed 13 Jan. 2020].

[xxi] Impostor Syndrome. (2020). *Everyone loses when bright people play small*. [online] Available at: https://impostorsyndrome.com/unpacking-michelle-obamas-impostor-syndrome/ [Accessed 20 Jan. 2020].

[xxii] Dalla-Camina, M. (2018). *The Reality of Imposter Syndrome*. [online] Psychology Today. Available at: https://www.psychologytoday.com/us/blog/real-women/201809/the-reality-imposter-syndrome [Accessed 15 Dec. 2019].

[xxiii] Healthline. (n.d.). *11 Signs and Symptoms of Anxiety Disorders*. [online] Available at: https://www.healthline.com/nutrition/anxiety-disorder-symptoms#section1 [Accessed 20 Dec. 2019].

[xxiv] Lifehack. (n.d.). *15 Simple Ways To Get Confidence Back*. [online] Available at: https://www.lifehack.org/articles/communication/15-simple-ways-get-confidence-back.html [Accessed 19 Dec. 2019].

[xxv] AGATHANGELOU, F. (2015). *Stop Comparing Yourself to Others to Improve Self-Esteem | HealthyPlace*. [online] Healthyplace.com. Available at: https://www.healthyplace.com/blogs/buildingselfesteem/2015/05/how-to-stop-comparing-yourself-to-others [Accessed 22 Dec. 2019].

[xxvi] Petersen, N. (2017). *The Dangers of Comparing Yourself to Others on Social Media | AllPsych Blog*. [online] AllPsych Blog. Available at: https://blog.allpsych.com/the-dangers-of-comparing-yourself-to-others-on-social-media/ [Accessed 22 Dec. 2019].

[xxvii] Bokhari, D. (2019). *You Are NOT Your Inner Dialogue*. [online] Meaningfulhq.com. Available at: https://www.meaningfulhq.com/you-are-not-your-inner-

dialogue.html [Accessed 24 Dec. 2019].

xxviii Ackerman, C. (2019). *What is Self-Worth and How Do We Increase it? (Incl. 4 Worksheets)*. [online] PositivePsychology.com. Available at: https://positivepsychology.com/self-worth/ [Accessed 3 Jan. 2020].

xxix Ackerman, C. (2019). *What is Self-Worth and How Do We Increase it? (Incl. 4 Worksheets)*. [online] PositivePsychology.com. Available at: https://positivepsychology.com/self-worth/ [Accessed 3 Jan. 2020].

xxx Goodreads.com. (2020). *Self Confidence Quotes (1311 quotes)*. [online] Available at: https://www.goodreads.com/quotes/tag/self-confidence [Accessed 13 Jan. 2020].

xxxi Edblad, P. (n.d.). *The Power of Small Wins: Why Celebrating Your Progress is Crucial for Long-Term Success – Patrik Edblad*. [online] Patrik Edblad. Available at: https://patrikedblad.com/self-discipline/the-power-of-small-wins/ [Accessed 6 Jan. 2020].

xxxii Goodreads.com. (2020). *Self Confidence Quotes (1311 quotes)*. [online] Available at: https://www.goodreads.com/quotes/tag/self-confidence [Accessed 13 Jan. 2020].

www.ingramcontent.com/pod-product-compliance
Lightning Source LLC
Chambersburg PA
CBHW020905080526
44589CB00011B/455